THE ART OF SERVING FOOD ATTRACTIVELY

The Art of
Serving Food Attractively

BY MARY ALBERT WENKER

ILLUSTRATED BY HELEN DISBROW

DOUBLEDAY & COMPANY, INC.

GARDEN CITY, NEW YORK

Contents

6　　*Contents*

Foreword

WHETHER the modern hostess is preparing a meal for her family or a luncheon for the afternoon bridge club, she knows that an attractive serving should be the rule and not the special exception. Food appeal depends upon its presentation. Colorful food imaginatively served will improve everybody's appetite, whereas a drab presentation of the same food may spoil the whole meal. *The Art of Serving Food Attractively* will prove to you that any one of your standard meals can be served in a new dress and bring exclamations of delight from all sides.

While family meals are important, there are other occasions where the hostess is expected to display her imagination in making food appealing. Preparing new, appetizing hors d'oeuvres and canapés for a cocktail party or making attractive individual salads for an afternoon luncheon is frequently a difficult task for the woman who entertains. After all there are only a limited number of things you can serve, so that the problem is to find new combinations and arrangements. Being a successful hostess is not a matter of luck; it is a matter of knowing how.

Art in serving is achieved by applying garnishes to foods, or using food combinations which harmonize in color, texture, and arrangement. I have not thought it necessary to write a complete recipe book, as most women have a favorite general cookbook in addition to their own standard recipes. However, in a few instances I have included the complete recipes in easy-to-follow steps.

With the garnishing and serving ideas I give in this book you will be able to create many interesting effects. After you have tried out these suggestions and witnessed the pleasure of your family or friends, and start to develop and use special decorating ideas of your own, you will have discovered the personal satisfaction that comes from serving beautiful food for all to enjoy.

THE ART OF SERVING FOOD ATTRACTIVELY

Rules for Garnishing

GARNISHING is an art—that can easily be acquired by following these few simple rules. It can be done with little or no additional time, effort, or money expenditure on the part of the culinary artist, and the results are far-reaching. Not only will the homemaker derive joy from the art, but the members of her family will sense the love and the thoughtfulness which prompted those extra little touches. Try it, and see for yourself.

1. Generally speaking, garnishes should be edible. However, there are a few exceptions, as will be seen in the following chapters.

2. Beauty is obtained through simplicity. Garnishes should appear natural, fresh, and dainty—never overworked or overdone.

3. All garnishes should be suitable in character and size to the food adorned. For example, a pickle fan would be out of place if served next to a piece of cake, just as a large calla-lily arrangement would be out of proportion on a small platter.

4. The flavor of edible garnishes should be in keeping with the food. Bland foods require more highly seasoned garnishes.

5. A few small groups of garnish are often more attractive than a continuous decorative scheme. For example, to carry out a Christmas theme around a salad mold, green-tinted mayonnaise may be fashioned into the shape of leaves with specks of candied cherry to simulate holly arranged at intervals instead of forming a continuous border. Elaborate wheels, flowers, chains, diamonds, or circles are lovely if carefully done. Use either whole or clean-cut pieces of fruit or vegetables and arrange in an orderly design around ring or loaf molds.

6. A garnish must be neatly arranged in a fashion that will enhance the food with which it is to be used. A flat-spreading garnish will make a mold appear smaller whereas perky lettuce will give it height.

7. Colors should harmonize—never clash. Small quantities of the more vivid natural colors may be used to accent a food. In using artificial coloring, great care must be exercised in producing tints that will be in keeping with the occasion and at the same time produce a pleasing effect rather than one which is repellent. Contrasting colors usually produce an artistic picture. So much of our food is neutral that a wide range of color treatment is permitted.

8. Garnishes which are too highly seasoned are not in good taste.

9. The serving dish as well as the garnish used must be considered. A beautiful dish serves as an accessory to the food. Do not hide it.

10. Temperature is a factor that will make or mar a garnish. To serve cold sliced frankfurters on a hot soup as a garnish would be most unsatisfactory. Any frozen food that is used as a garnish should be sufficiently cold to hold its shape.

11. The consistencies of garnish and food can be contrasted with excellent results, such as sauce over molded food.

12. Garnishes need not be expensive. Properly used, almost any leftover material can do wonders to make a drab or uninteresting dish take on a regal aspect.

13. Garnishes should not be used to disguise deficiencies or food of poor quality.

14. The setting must be viewed as a whole. Harmonious plate or platter arrangements can be ruined if they clash with the table color scheme or the lighting of the room.

MATERIALS

Materials commonly used for garnishes are limited, but the ways in which they may be applied are legion. Garnishing tools used may be few or many. However, a culinary artist will extend her art considerably with a greater variety of gadgets. Tools generally used are:

1. *Knives*
   With blunt, round, or curved blades
   With sharp-pointed blades
   With fluting edge
   Shrimp rod and scoop (often called shrimp cutter)
   French fruit or vegetable cutters
   Vegetable friller
   A ¼-inch peeler
   French butter curler
   Fancy cutters
   Cookie cutters of various shapes
2. *Small wire baskets for deep-fat frying*
3. *Rosette irons*
4. *Timbale irons—tiny and average sizes*
5. *Melon or bomb molds*
6. *Individual small molds*
7. *Pastry syringe with tubes*
8. *Pastry bag with tubes*
9. *Egg slicer; fruit and vegetable slicers*
10. *Pastry jagger*
11. *Pastry crimper*
12. *Pastry designer*
13. *Grapefruit scalloper*
14. *Paintbrush and pure fruit and vegetable dyes*

HELPFUL HINTS

How to Use a Cardboard Stencil   Cut a piece of medium-stiff cardboard in the shape but slightly larger than the food to be decorated. Trace a design or the outline of some specific object on the cardboard and cut out the design with scissors or a razor blade in a safety holder. The design should be clean-cut, with no ragged edges.

If the food to be decorated is dry or firm, the cardboard stencil can rest on the surface; if it is soft and moist, hold the stencil a fraction of an inch above the surface. Sprinkle the garnish over the design, making sure that all parts of the design are completely filled in.

Remove the stencil carefully without disturbing the design.

How to Frost a Glass   To frost glass stemware, brush the rim of each glass with lemon juice or slightly beaten egg white. Dip the rim in powdered sugar and let dry. If necessary, dip a second or third time.

How to Unmold Gelatin   Dip the mold in warm water long enough for the gelatin to loosen. If necessary, loosen the edges with a thin knife. Place the serving plate over the mold and invert. If the gelatin does not come out immediately, wrap a hot towel around the form and after a few seconds give the mold a hard shake.

How to Use Fruit or Vegetable Coloring   Pure fruit or vegetable coloring can be purchased in liquid or powdered form. The coloring should be added a little at a time, mixing thoroughly after each addition, until the desired shade is obtained. Add coloring to the ingredients in the liquid state (that is, before whipping or freezing).

To tint solid foods (such as pears or hard-cooked eggs), add the coloring to water or sirup and then place the food in the colored solution until it becomes the right shade.

Solid foods can also be painted by using the pure fruit or vegetable dyes. A paintbrush should be kept especially for use in the kitchen.

How to Make a Paper Pastry Tube   Use a stiff sheet of paper (8"×11") and roll into a funnel. To prevent the funnel from unrolling, fasten with gummed tape. Cut off as much of the tip as is necessary for the size of opening desired. Fill the funnel about two-thirds full and force through the tip by squeezing the large end of the funnel.

Appetizers

ALMONDS Place blanched toasted almonds in petal arrangements on buttered rounds of white, Boston brown, or fruit breads.

Tint cream cheese a delicate pink with vegetable or fruit coloring. Add chopped pimento, then mold in the shape of almonds about ¼ inch thick. Press a blanched toasted almond on each side of the cheese molds.

Insert a blanched toasted almond on long edge in spread on a cracker or toast strip.

ANCHOVIES Fasten a rolled anchovy fillet on top of a one-inch square of cheese with a pretzel stick just before serving. (Stick will soften if allowed to stand too long.)

With pastry tube pipe anchovy paste on rye krisp criss-cross fashion and around the edge. To make anchovy paste, cream 2 tablespoons butter and add ½ teaspoon paste as purchased; or rub yolks of 2 hard-cooked eggs to a smooth paste. Combine 2 boned and mashed anchovies and ¼ cup butter. Mix with egg yolks and add few grains of paprika.

Spread finger strips of white or whole-wheat bread with anchovy paste. Form border with caviar or arrange caviar in parallel lines across bread strip.

With pastry tube press a rosette of anchovy paste on top of a scored cucumber slice. Top with a tiny piece of truffle, parsley, or watercress.

Cut toasted bread into 1½" squares and spread with snappy cheese. Top with slice of hard-cooked egg and a rolled anchovy. Or place rolled anchovy directly on top of cheese spread and place chopped egg yolk border around anchovy.

APRICOT BALLS   Combine 1 cup of ground dried apricots (or ½ cup apricots and ½ cup pitted prunes), ½ cup of coconut (long shreds, white or tinted), ½ cup chopped nut meats, ½ tablespoon grated orange rind, and enough orange juice to hold ingredients together. Form into balls or other shapes; roll in powdered sugar. These balls should not be much larger than marbles.

ASPIC Cubes   Use your favorite aspic recipe. When the gelatin is dissolved, add vegetable or fruit coloring—red, orange, yellow, or green. Pour into a large flat pan. (The gelatin should be about 1 inch deep.) When firm, cut in cubes. Place assorted colored cubes in tiny timbale cases.

Shred congealed aspic, combining different colors. Place in tiny patty shells or on potato chips.

Coating   With a teaspoon pour colored aspic in a thin coating over completed canapés. This will give a shiny effect and preserve the canapés. Be sure the aspic is just beginning to congeal when it is poured over appetizer.

Cut aspic jelly in fancy shapes. Place anchovy or sardine on top of jelly. Jellied aspic may be placed on lettuce, cracker, or bread foundation.

BACON Cut slices of bacon in half, spread with cheese relish and chopped pickle. Roll up securely, fasten with toothpick, and broil slowly. Drain and serve hot.

Grill thin slices of bacon. Place tiny bacon curls on top of cheese-covered muffin slice or other foundation. Surround with tiny pearl onions.

Spread oblong pieces of bread with processed cheese; arrange two small slices of bacon on top in form of letter X; grill, remove from broiler, and place two stuffed olives, one on each side of center of bacon cross.

Wrap small slices of bacon around olives and fasten with toothpicks; grill slowly; serve hot.

Tiny bits of grilled bacon make attractive and tasty borders on canapés.

BEEF Chop dried beef very fine. Mold cream cheese into balls, then roll each ball in chopped dried beef, coating completely. Insert a toothpick in each cream-cheese ball and stick into a grapefruit, orange, or Edam cheese ball in center of appetizer tray.

Spread strips of dried beef or other cuts of cold, well-seasoned meat with cheese. Roll tightly, chill, slice crosswise, and serve on toothpicks. When using larger slices of meat, spread a second slice with cheese and roll around the first one. Chill and slice.

BEETS Hollow out very small cooked beets about the size of walnuts. Fill with horse-radish.

Hold a small cooked beet on a toothpick. Form rose petals around beet by forcing cream cheese which has been tinted a delicate yellow through pastry tube. Start at the top of the beet and work around to base, being sure to overlap each petal. Fasten roses to grapefruit, orange, or apple, whatever is used in center of appetizer tray, by inserting toothpick into centerpiece.

Top a slice of pickled beet with a small green pepper ring which has been stuffed with pimento cheese.

Fill small hollowed-out pickled beets with any highly seasoned cheese, fish, or meat mixture. Top with a tiny sprig of parsley.

BOLOGNA AND CHEESE TRI-ANGLES Spread 3 slices of fine bologna with horse-radish mustard and stack alternately with 2 slices of aged cheese cut ⅛ inch thick. Use a 3-inch round cutter to trim to shape. Remnants may be used in sandwich spreads, vegetable salads, or macaroni dishes. Stick 10 toothpicks equidistant through the bologna stack to hold it together. Cut into pie-shaped wedges with one pick per wedge.

BOUQUET APPETIZERS Assorted appetizers on toothpicks such as pickled onions, stuffed olives, a square of grilled cervelat, Braunschweiger balls, and cornucopias. Cheese frills and other appetizers served on toothpicks may also be included. The toothpicks are held together and pushed through the center of a small paper doily. The doily is then gathered around the appetizers and fastened to the toothpicks with gummed tape.

BRAUNSCHWEIGER BALLS   Mash Braunschweiger (smoked) liver sausage. Place a pat of liver sausage in the palm of your hand. Add a small pimento olive and wrap and roll to cover. Roll in minced parsley for color and flavor and to prevent sausage from drying. To mince parsley quickly, hold over a glass and cut with scissors.

BUTTER   Soften sweet or salted butter and tint any shade desired. Using pastry tube, pipe around or on top of any selected foundation, or form flowers or other objects on canapés.

CAPERS   Cut pickled capers in slices or pieces and arrange in design on crackers which have been spread with sardine paste.

CAVIAR   Use rounds of bread about 1½ to 1¾ inches in diameter for a foundation. Dip in beaten egg and milk, as for French toast, and sauté. Spread with red and black caviar in an arrangement of alternating circles from outer edge to center. Cover with aspic. When set, decorate with savory butter forced through a pastry tube.

Cut stuffed eggs in half lengthwise. Arrange a bit of red caviar at one end and black caviar at the other end of egg on cut surface.

Spread muffin slices with seasoned caviar and top with a cucumber slice marinated in a sweet-sour pickle solution. Cut a small piece of beet in desired shape (such as star, diamond, et cetera) and place on top of cucumber. Arrange capers around the beet. Top with a pearl onion.

Place ½ teaspoon of black caviar in center of cheese-covered crackers and around edge to form border.

CELERY Cut tops from a bunch of celery; separate, then wash and dry the stalks. Stuff the stalks with pimento-cream cheese spread. Press the next larger stalk onto the smallest. Continue with all the cheese-filled stalks, pressing onto the last until all the pieces from one stalk have been used. Tie with string; chill, then slice.

CENTERPIECES Interesting centerpieces that may be used for a large tray of appetizers:

Completely surround a grapefruit, an orange, or a mold of Edam cheese with cream-cheese balls which have been rolled in chopped dried beef and held in place with toothpicks.

Arrange rows of appetizers served on toothpicks alternately over base or form a design with different types of appetizers.

A porcupine centerpiece may be made in the following manner. Using a grapefruit as a base and toothpicks as quills, force each toothpick through the appetizer far enough to hold it firmly in the grapefruit. The opposite ends will stick out like porcupine quills. Insert a row of stuffed olives across the top and down the sides of the grapefruit. Along the top and parallel with the olives put 7 or 8 anchovies. Finish these rows with cubes of American and Swiss cheese of approximately the same size as the anchovies. Continue with rows of cheese to cover the entire grapefruit. Finish the porcupine by using 2 anchovies for the eyes.

Doll Centerpiece   Use a lady china figurine for the base. This can usually be purchased in the five-and-ten. Separate the leaves from a head of lettuce; arrange around the figurine in the form of a skirt and fasten together with toothpicks. Cut flowers out of thin slices of bread, turnips, rutabagas, or carrots, using a scalloped cutter.  Place pieces of truffle or carrot circles in the center of white flowers and truffle or turnips for the center of yellow flowers. Attach with toothpicks to the lettuce skirt. Fasten sprigs of parsley or watercress at the waist and an inch or two down one side.

CERVELAT CHIPS   Have cervelat cut paper thin. Lay on broiler rack, and broil quickly. Turn, and lightly brown other side. Crispy, zippy, and delicious.

CHEESE   Cubes   Cut cheese in ¾-inch cubes. Cut a stuffed olive in half lengthwise and fasten to cheese cube with a toothpick or pretzel stick.

Place a ¼-inch cube of cheese between the 2 halves of a stuffed olive which has been cut crosswise. Fasten with toothpicks.

Mix Roquefort cheese with enough cream to give it the consistency of cream cheese. Serve on toast or cracker foundation; top with tiny pearl onions or chopped sweet-sour pickles arranged in a design.

Combine cream cheese, chopped dates or raisins and nut meats. Add a drop of lemon juice. Spread on wafers and top with a flower made with sections of dates and an orange-rind center.

Mix cream cheese, chopped nuts, minced sweet-sour

pickles, and preserved watermelon rind. If desired, use grated onion or other spicy relish to suit taste. Spread paste on finger strips of Boston brown bread. Pipe with white or tinted cheese to carry out seasonal color scheme. To tint cheese, add pure fruit or vegetable coloring.

Add a little horse-radish to cream cheese and moisten with prepared mustard or chili sauce. Fill potato chips or the holes of small pretzels with this mixture. Top with bits of red radish or make tiny rosettes by forcing the cheese spread through a tube.

Blend any of the popular cheese relishes with mayonnaise or Thousand Island dressing. Serve on split halves of tiny baking-powder biscuits. Sprinkle shaved Brazil nuts over the top. Crown with a delicate pink rose which is made with a decorating tube. Use tinted cream cheese for both the rose and its leaves. Tiny mint leaves may be used in place of the cheese tinted green.

Tint softened cream cheese with pure fruit or vegetable coloring. Pipe around edges of canapés, or form flowers, leaves, or other designs with the various tubes in a decorating set. A marbled effect can be obtained by placing two colors of cheese next to each other in the decorating tube.

Balls Form balls from grated American cheese or processed cheese. Serve plain on toothpicks or roll in chopped parsley, chopped or ground nut meats, caviar, chipped beef, or paprika. Cream cheese may be used in a similar way.

Other cheese molds Mold grated American cheese or processed cheese in shape of pumpkins, apples, strawberries, carrots, or other fruits and vegetables. Tint surface of molded objects with fruit or vegetable coloring applied with a pastry brush. To make a cheese apple, sprinkle paprika on one side of cheese mold, insert whole clove at blossom end, and a crab-apple stem at the other end. To make a cheese carrot, mold and fasten a sprig of parsley at large end of cheese carrot.

Tint cream cheese green, combine with chopped pistachio

nuts, spread on very thin slices of bread, roll like jelly roll, and slice just before serving. Place a tiny rosette of cream cheese in the center. Make the rosette by forcing cheese through a pastry tube; garnish with mint leaves.

CHERRIES Bing cherries, candied cherries, or maraschino cherries may be used whole, halved, or cut in sections, and arranged on appetizer or canapé to form flowers or geometric designs. Both candied and maraschino cherries may be obtained in red or green colors.

Place whole cherry in tiny timbale case.

Pit cherries. Beginning from open end cut petals down to but not through the center at the other end. Spread out on canapé. Use strips of citron for stem and leaves.

Cut the upper half of a green maraschino cherry into eighths by cutting halfway down through the cherry so that the lower half remains intact. Do the same with a red maraschino cherry. Place the red cherry within the green one and use this way as a garnish, or place a tiny piece of candied orange peel in the center of the flower that is formed.

CHOWCHOW Cut an outline design in a piece of cardboard which is about the size of the canapés to be used. Place this cardboard stencil over a canapé which has been covered with a tasty spread. Fill the outline design with chowchow, then gently lift the cardboard and you will have a perfect picture.

CHUTNEY Make small onion cups by hollowing out centers of parboiled onions, then fill with chutney.

Cover thin slices of cooked ham with chopped chutney, roll, and fasten with toothpicks.

CLAMS   Cut squares of bread 2″ × 1¼″. Scoop out enough of the center of the foundation to hold 2 tiny clams. Place clams, which have first been marinated in tart tomato sauce, in the basket thus formed. Pipe around edge with savory butter and place a sprig of watercress at one end.

Hollow out tiny cooked beets to form cups and fill with chopped cooked clams.

Serve deviled clams on clam shell.

CRAB MEAT   Deep-fat fry crab meat, flake, and mix with mushroom sauce. Serve in tiny cream-puff shells.

CUCUMBERS   Score cucumber, slice, and marinate in French dressing. Make slits about ⅓ to ½ inch apart in red radish of average size. Drain cucumber slices shortly before using and insert in cuts in radishes.

CURRANTS   Scatter dried currants over canapé.

Form a border around half an egg which has been stuffed with the deviled yolk.

DATES   Chop dates and scatter over surface of appetizer.

Cut dates in sections, arrange petal fashion on canapé.

Stuff dates, then slice. Overlap slices on nut or fruit-bread foundation which has been covered with a savory spread.

Cut foundation in octagon shape, and cover with a suitable spread. Place date strips on foundation so that each strip radiates out from the center to each point on the octagon.

EGGS Sieve the yolk and the white of hard-cooked eggs separately or together. Sprinkle over surface of appetizer.

Mash the yolk of a hard-cooked egg, mix with mayonnaise, and use as a spread or piping material.

Cut hard-cooked eggs in half, remove yolks and put them through a sieve. To each dozen eggs add 2 tablespoons cream or mayonnaise, 1 tablespoon vinegar, 1½ teaspoons mustard, 1½ teaspoons Worcestershire sauce, ¾ teaspoon salt, and ¼ teaspoon pepper. Other seasonings, such as onion juice, caviar, anchovies, ham, sardine, or cheese may be added as desired. Fill egg-white halves with deviled mixture.

Fill centers of hard-cooked egg whites with red cabbage coleslaw which has been cut fine and well seasoned.

Spread thin slices of dried beef with seasoned egg-yolk mixture. Roll into a thin roll, chill, and slice before serving.

Form tiny balls from mashed egg yolk or whole egg mixed with mayonnaise. Roll in finely minced parsley, chives, caviar, or paprika. Serve on wafers or toothpicks.

Cut hard-cooked eggs in sections, sprinkle with salt; top with alternate strips of pimento and green pepper, or cut designs out of pimento and green pepper and arrange artistically on the egg sections.

Cut hard-cooked egg whites into stars, crescents, clubs, or other shapes; place on foundation which has been spread with dark savory topping.

Egg Boats Use rectangular-shaped foundation and hard-cooked eggs cut lengthwise and prepared as stuffed eggs. Place half an egg on each foundation which has been covered with Roquefort-cheese spread. Cut a sprig of parsley to represent a sail and stand upright in each "boat." Sail may

also be made from flaked white meat of tuna fish. Form a yacht with two or three sails of different heights.

Slice a hard-cooked egg. Top with stars or other objects cut out of pimento. Place on small round of brown bread ¼" thick. Use bits of pimento to form border around egg slice on bread foundation. Use marinated truffle or mushroom caps around egg slice instead of pimento, if desired.

Place a slice of tinted pickled egg on small rounds of toast or other foundation which has been covered with a tasty spread.

Cover a shaped foundation with egg-salad spread. Form border of chopped parsley and place a piece of truffle in the center. Truffle may be cut to resemble some specific object.

FISH Mix crab meat with lemon juice and spread on crackers. Top with a slice of cucumber; pipe with tinted mayonnaise.

Combine salmon, chopped pimento, chopped stuffed olives, and enough mayonnaise to moisten. Serve on potato chips or on small baking-powder biscuits. Top with bits of truffle.

Serve grilled sardines on finger-strip pieces of toast.

Shred fish flesh which has been freed from bones. Add enough mayonnaise to hold fish together, form into balls, roll in chopped parsley, chopped olives, paprika, or sieved egg yolk.

Remove black vein from the back of boiled shelled shrimp. Pipe tinted cheese in cavity made by removing vein. Arrange the shrimp in rosette formation or hang over edge of vegetable cup which is made from turnip, carrot, onion, or other suitable vegetable. Serve shrimp sauce in the vegetable cup.

Wrap a whole oyster in a strip of bacon. Grill. Sprinkle with chopped parsley and serve on toothpick.

Serve fried oysters on top of tiny baking-powder biscuits.

FLOWERS　Place a fresh blossom at base of stemware containing appetizer. (Or use a cluster of small blossoms.) Arrange suitable leaves with the flowers.

Float a fresh flower on a slice of lemon or lime. Pull the stem of the flower far enough through a hole in center of the slice to stabilize flower. Float in fruit cocktail or punch bowl.

Arrange tiny corsages of flowers on appetizer tray.

FRANKFURTERS　Grill tiny whole frankfurters. Serve on toothpicks.

Slice hot frankfurters. Insert in tiny muffins and serve immediately.

Heat tiny frankfurters in barbecued sauce, and serve in small patty shells or timbale cases.

FRUIT　Berries　Blackberries, blueberries, loganberries, raspberries, thimbleberries, strawberries.

Scatter berries (one or more varieties) over ice or sherbet made of the same fruit.

Place a cluster of berries on the edge of a glass or on the serving plate at the base of glass stemware. Arrange a few of the natural leaves with the tiny cluster of fruit. Be sure to wash and drain berries and leaves well before using.

Use whole strawberries, with or without hulls and stems, and serve plain or dipped in powdered sugar.

Arrange sectioned or sliced strawberries artistically on top of fruit cocktails.

Grapefruit　Arrange grapefruit sections in petal fashion on lettuce and place maraschino cherry or stuffed prune in center of each flower formed. Use as a border on a large appetizer tray.

Grapes Separate a bunch of Concord or other grapes into small clusters. Wash grapes, drain well, and balance a cluster on the rim of each glass of fruit cocktail. Have part of the cluster fall inside the glass, the other part (usually the larger section) fall outside the glass. Use either tiny grape leaves or a sprig of mint with the grapes. Grape clusters may also be placed on a serving plate at the base of glass stemware.

Frosted Grapes Separate a large bunch of grapes into smaller clusters. Dip clusters into an egg white that has been beaten until frothy. Shake off surplus egg white and dip grapes into powdered sugar. The egg white will absorb the coat of sugar. Dip the clusters into the powdered sugar until grapes are pure white and completely covered. Dry on wire rack. Place frosted grapes at base of stemware which contains fruit cocktail. Intermingle each cluster with small grape leaves if in season, or use any suitable leaf for foliage. For variation place frosted grape clusters at the rim of the cocktail glass so that one or two grapes hang over the side of the glass.

Lemons Place a small slice of lemon or lime on the rim of a glass. For variation, remove pulp from half a slice, curl, then fasten on rim of glass.

Oranges Use same as lemon or lime slice or cut in geometric shapes. Candied orange peel may be cut into many shapes.

Pineapple Roll outer edge of canned pineapple wedge in chopped mint leaves and fasten to rim of glass containing orange, lemon, or lime sherbet. For variation place 3 of these wedges on top of sherbet so that the points of the wedges meet.

Plums Cut a prune plum into sections. Arrange petal fashion on round foundation of fruit bread. Or place plum petals on top of fruit cocktail.

Use sections of plum as a border, scallop fashion, on suitable foundation.

Prunes Stuff a cooked prune with cheese, nut meats, orange section, marshmallow, or any other suitable filling. Serve on toothpick or on tiny leaf of lettuce.

FRUIT ICE OR SHERBET Place a scoop of apricot, black raspberry, mint, orange, or tinted green-gage plum ice on top of melon balls or fresh or canned fruit. Add ginger ale just before serving. A sprig of mint may be placed near the rim of glass.

GARNISH PASTE Cream 4 tablespoons butter; gradually add an equal amount of tomato paste or hard-cooked egg yolks which have been rubbed through a sieve. Season with tomato sauce, onion juice, a little prepared mustard, salt, and pepper. Force through a pastry tube to form designs and borders on canapés.

GINGER Cut preserved ginger into strips and arrange in designs on a nut-bread foundation covered with a cheese spread.

Chop preserved ginger. Place a cardboard stencil over a foundation covered with a tasty spread. Fill outline with the chopped ginger. Remove cardboard.

JELLY Drop bits of jelly or marmalade in center of canapé.

KUMQUATS Cut peel of kumquats into four petals, being careful not to cut through the inner skin. Free the peel from pulp without breaking or tearing either one. Soak in ice water. Petals will curl back in shape of flower. Place on bed of greens on appetizer tray.

LIVER   Cook liver balls and roll in chopped chipped beef or chopped parsley. Serve on toothpicks or in tiny patty shells or timbale cases.

LOBSTER   Place well-seasoned lobster meat in cucumber boat or in lemon basket. To make a cucumber boat, cut a thin slice from long side of a small cucumber. Remove pulp from the larger section of the cucumber; shape carved out portion to resemble boat.

Cut hard-cooked eggs in half lengthwise and remove yolk. Fill cavities of eggs with chopped lobster meat which has been mixed with mayonnaise or tartar sauce. Place on a nest of shredded lettuce or on sautéed oval-shaped slice of bread. Pipe colored butter over egg to suit color scheme. Place a sprig of watercress at base of egg.

MAYONNAISE   Pipe pure mayonnaise (that is stiff enough to hold its shape) on canapés or salad appetizers.

Tint mayonnaise any color needed for color theme. Force through pastry tube to form rosettes, leaves, or other designs.

Use butter or a hydrogenated shortening in making salad dressing. Follow recipe for making mayonnaise but substitute butter or hydrogenated shortening in place of oil. The butter or shortening must be liquid when added. The mayonnaise will become firm upon standing. Cut in balls, cubes, fingers, stars, or any other fancy shapes. This dressing may be tinted by adding fruit or vegetable coloring while the fat is still liquid.

MELONS   Peel a honeydew melon and cut in half. Remove the seeds and membrane. Cut a slice of melon about one inch thick for a melon ring and flute the outer edge. Place in center of appetizer tray. With a French ball cutter cut balls from watermelon, muskmelon, and honeydew melon. Fill the center of the melon ring with the balls and decorate with sprigs of mint. Grapes may be used together with melon rings to form an attractive garnish. Use any variety in season. Cut grapes in half and place on the honeydew ring to form a border of tiny grape clusters. As a variation, arrange frosted grapes at intervals on the melon rings.

MINT   Arrange separate leaves or sprigs of mint on canapés or other appetizers.

Sprinkle chopped mint leaves over canapés or use to form border or other design. The edges of appetizers may also be dipped into the chopped mint.

Line glasses with sprigs or leaves of mint. Add melon balls which have been tinted or left in their natural color. Pour wine-flavored fruit juice over balls. Add a dash of cinnamon or mace.

NUT MEATS   Spread two large pecan or walnut halves with cream-cheese relish and press them together.

Roll cheese balls in chopped pistachio nut meats.

Sprinkle chopped nut meats over foundation which has been covered with a tasty spread.

Shave Brazil nut meats into lengthwise slices. Place petal fashion on foundation and place a cherry in the center.

OLIVES   Roll a ripe, green, or stuffed olive in strip of bacon and broil until bacon is crisp. Serve on toothpicks.

Remove pimento from a stuffed olive; refill cavity with anchovy paste, chopped nut meats, or whole blanched and toasted almonds.

Stuff large olives with a sharp cheese, wrap on bacon strip, and broil until bacon is crisp. Serve hot on toothpicks.

ONIONS Slice a sweet onion, separate the rings, and use plain or tinted. To tint, allow rings to stand in water or pickle solution which has been colored with pure fruit or vegetable dye.

Parboil onions and scoop out center to form onion cups. Refill with a colorful relish or tiny hot meat balls.

Pickle small onions or onion rings by marinating them in a sweet-sour pickle solution.

Arrange pearl onions as a border around canapés or form other designs or dividing lines.

PAPRIKA Sprinkle paprika over entire surface of canapé or over a cardboard stencil, or dip edges in paprika which has been sprinkled on a plate.

PARSLEY Arrange sprigs of parsley where an accent of green is needed.

Sprinkle chopped parsley over an appetizer or roll balls or other molds in it. To mince parsley quickly, hold the bunch of parsley over a glass and cut with scissors.

PEPPERS Tiny red or green peppers may be stuffed with cream cheese, chilled, and then cut in slices or sections.

Fill small pepper cups with any piquant dressing and arrange on appetizer tray.

Slice peppers. Remove seeds. Overlap rings or use sections of rings to form geometric designs.

Chop peppers, and use as border or center design.

PICKLES Slice sweet-sour pickles, then cut slices in wedges and arrange in star shape on top of cheese spread wafers.

Cut sweet-sour pickles in strips, place on octagon-shaped foundation with each pickle strip radiating from center of bread to each point in the octagon.

Make a pickle fan by slashing lengthwise slices in a small pickle. Be sure not to cut through the stem end of the pickle, as this forms the base. Press base with thumb and forefinger and slices of pickle will spread fan-shaped. Cut a slit in the top of a radish large enough to hold the pickle fan and insert the pickle.

Minced Pickles Place cardboard stencil over suitable foundation which has been covered with savory butter or shrimp paste. Cover stencil design with the minced pickles. Lift the cardboard carefully.

Roll a dry sweet-sour pickle in cream cheese then in a layer of smoked salmon. Fasten with a toothpick. Serve whole or cut in crosswise sections.

Cut a slice from one end of a medium-sized dill pickle; remove center with an apple corer. Drain and fill with cheese-relish spread. Chill, then cut crosswise slices.

Pickle Boats Use small sweet pickles. Cut a slice from the bottom of each pickle to steady the boats. Cut a wedge out of the upper or top part of the pickle boat and fill it with cream-cheese relish. To make a sail, cut a pie-shaped wedge of salami. Insert the rounded part of the wedge into cream cheese so that the point will stand upright. The pickle boat may also be filled with pearl onions.

Cut a slice from one end of a dill pickle. Remove center with an apple corer. Drain out as much liquid as possible. Fill center with tinted cream cheese or cheese-relish spread. Chill for an hour, then cut crosswise into ½-inch slices. May be decorated with caviar.

Select large dill pickles; cut each pickle into thin crosswise slices. Cut three fourths through the diameter of each slice. Cross the ends over to form a miniature cornucopia and fasten with half a toothpick. Fill with a cheese spread which has been softened at room temperature and forced through a pastry tube.

PIMENTO   Cut pimento into strips, stars, or other designs. Place on canapés.

Chop pimento and arrange in design on bread foundation covered with a tasty spread. Use cardboard stencil.

RADISHES   Score a red radish, cut in slices, insert in small cucumber gashed at intervals.

Radish roses, tulips, and fans   Use small red radishes. Cut off the tip of the root and all but a small piece of the stem. With a thin sharp knife score the radish and cut as illustrated. Radishes will stay crisp and petals or fan will open if they are kept in ice water until ready to serve.

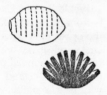

RAISINS   Use for color contrast or for accent. Use singly or in groups on canapés or hors d'oeuvres.

RELISH Spread a foundation with cranberry and orange relish, top with a slice of stuffed olive, and surround with pearl onions. A white star cut from hard-cooked egg white may be placed in center of canapé.

Use a crescent-shaped bread foundation. Place green relish on one half of the foundation and red relish on the other half. Other color combinations may be used, such as green and white, and red and white. Alternate spreads of spiced apricot and prune pulp. Spread black and red caviar alternately around edge of crescent which has been spread with tasty relish. Any number of color and flavor combinations may be used to suit the occasion.

Spread thin slices of cold chipped beef, ham, or tongue with a tart relish. Roll and fasten with a toothpick.

Stuff celery with a cheese relish or with a mixture made by combining peanut butter, chopped cooked ham, and pearl onions. Cut stuffed celery, place on toothpicks or on bits of lettuce or crackers.

SALAMI Tiny cornucopias are made from small cervelat or salami. Cut thin slices. Slash to center of each slice with scissors. Roll into cone shape and fasten with toothpick. Soften cream cheese by combining with melted butter and season with horse-radish mustard. Fill the salami cones with the cream-cheese spread, using the tip of a knife or pastry tube.

TOMATOES Cut small tomatoes into ¼-inch slices. Serve raw or broiled.

Top tomato slice with truffles or mushroom caps.

Arrange a green pepper circle on top of a slice of tomato. Place a stuffed olive in the center of pepper ring and surround the olive with pearl onions. Serve on crackers of same size or on bread foundation.

Tomato Cheese Rose Use a firm tomato about the size of a walnut. Wash and dry. Soften cream cheese and tint a delicate yellow or pink. Fill the pointed half of a teaspoon with cream cheese and level with a knife or spatula. To form the petals, hold the teaspoon against the side of the tomato;  press the cheese onto the tomato with a downward stroke of the spoon. Place sieved egg yolk in the center of the flower. Chill in refrigerator before serving. Arrange on a tray of appetizers.

Beverages

BERRIES Blueberries, blackberries, loganberries, raspberries, strawberries, or thimbleberries. Serve whole berries singly or in small groups on top of whipped cream or on scoops of ice cream floating in beverage. Place whole berries on lemon or lime slices floating in fruit beverages.

BANANAS Slice bananas and dip in fruit juice. Place overlapping slices on top of a thick banana float in stem glasses or tall glasses. Top with whipped cream and sprinkle with a few grains of nutmeg.

CANDIES Sprinkle tiny decorative candies over whipped cream or on surface of light-colored beverage just before serving.

CHERRIES Use green or red candied cherries. Place a half cherry or a whole cherry with or without stem on top of whipped cream or ice cream ball, or float on orange or other fruit slice on top of beverage.

Cut fresh or candied cherry in petal shapes and arrange in shape of flower on top of whipped cream, ice cream, or fruit slices.

Maraschino cherries may be used in the same way as above. They may also be cut into strips or dots and geometric patterns to be used as borders, or placed in the center or on the sides of floating ice cream or whipped cream.

Hang a small cluster of Bing cherries on rim of glass, or float on fruit slices.

Place a cluster of fresh cherries with leaves at the base of a glass on a serving plate.

CHOCOLATE   Pour melted chocolate over whipped cream or ice-cream balls floating in beverage. This garnish is particularly effective on coffee or chocolate drinks.

Sprinkle chocolate shot over whipped cream.

An attractive way to garnish a banana cream shake or other white frothy beverage is to pour 1 tablespoon chocolate sirup down into the beverage at a point about a fourth inch from the edge of the glass; repeat on opposite side of the glass. Stir just enough to give marbled effect.

COCONUT   Sprinkle short or long shreds of white coconut on tinted whipped cream or directly on surface of beverage.

Scatter short or long shreds of tinted coconut on white whipped cream. Coconut may be purchased colored or it may be tinted at home.

CREAM   Pour thin cream over dark frothy beverages.

Use whipped cream as a garnish and top with:

1. *Cherries*
2. *Coconut, white or tinted*
3. *Colored candies*
4. *Chocolate shot or sirup, or melted chocolate which will harden in any shape formed*
5. *Banana slices*
6. *Spice (nutmeg, mace, cinnamon, or other flavor desired); use spice sparingly*
7. *Tangerine sections*

Whipping cream may be tinted with pure fruit or vegetable coloring. Dissolve coloring in cream before beating. Force whipped cream through decorating tube to form flowers or other designs.

CURRANTS   Select bright red clusters of fresh currants with leaves. Wash, dry, and arrange on rim of glass containing beverage, or place at base of glass on serving plate.

Place currants on frothy beverages either singly or in groups to form border or other design.

FROSTED GLASS   See Helpful Hints.

GINGER   Mince preserved ginger; scatter directly over beverage or over whipped cream on top of beverage.

GRAPES   Place bunches of assorted grapes with their leaves on top of an ice block in punch bowl. Hollow the top of the ice block slightly to hold grapes in place.

Arrange tiny clusters of seedless grapes on rim of glass with natural grape leaves or mint leaves.

ICE CREAM   Homemade ice cream may be tinted any desired shade by adding pure fruit or vegetable coloring to the liquid cream before freezing. Since ice cream will freeze to a lighter shade, tint cream a shade darker than needed. Freeze ice cream to a mushy consistency. Pour into various shaped molds which have been lined with waxed paper, and freeze. Remove from molds and paint each according to object it represents with a paintbrush reserved for fruit dye.

Cut tinted ice cream in cubes; scatter over whipped cream on beverage.

ICE CUBES   Use part of the liquid needed for the beverage; freeze slowly. Suitable liquids are:

Cider
Coffee brew
Ginger ale or other carbonated beverage
Lemonade or orangeade
Water. Use plain or tint any color desired, but remem-ber that delicate tints are most attractive. The water may be flavored to harmonize with the color as, for example, oil of peppermint to flavor green-tinted water.

A garnish may be frozen into or onto ice cubes. Cubes should be frozen slowly to prevent expansion and cloudiness. For best results follow these few simple directions: Fill ice cube tray about one third full with water or other liquid. Freeze partially; add the garnish; freeze again. This will hold the garnish in place. Add liquid until tray is three fourths full, then finish freezing. Suitable fruits or leaves are

Berries
Candied fruit
Cherries—Bing, maraschino, mint
Grapes
Lemon slice, quartered
Lime slice, quartered
Mint leaves
Orange slice, quartered
Pineapple cubes
Strawberry—whole or sliced
Watercress

To freeze leaves on the surface of cube, place leaves on the ice cubes and cover with enough water to form a thin coat of ice when frozen. Return to freezing compartment until ready to use.

JELLY Place a small cube of jelly on top of whipped cream or in center of frothy jelly punch.

LEMONS Float a slice of lemon on top of beverage. For variation, stud the slice with whole cloves; sprinkle with chopped preserved ginger or fruit peel; or float a fresh blossom on the lemon slice.

Cut lemon rind in the shape of stars and float on beverage.

Flute the rind of a whole lemon; slice. Make a cut through rind and pulp to the center of each slice. Place over rim of tall glass either alone or with a sprig of mint.

Place a half or whole cherry on top of a slice of lemon. Cherry may also be cut to resemble a flower.

Insert a colored toothpick through a whole strawberry, a lemon or an orange slice, and another whole strawberry. Place over rim of glass.

LIMES Use the same as lemon.

MACAROON CRUMBS Sprinkle over whipped cream or ice cream floating in beverage.

MARSHMALLOWS Float a white or a tinted marshmallow in a glass of punch.

Place a marshmallow in each cup and pour hot chocolate or cocoa over it to fill cup. Marshmallow will float on top.

MINT   Float a sprig of mint together with a cherry in a beverage.

Arrange sprigs of mint on edge of glass.

Fasten leaves in an orange or lemon slice and float in beverage.

NUTS   Sprinkle chopped nut meats over whipped cream or a scoop of ice cream floating in a glass of Orange Frost or other cooling drink.

ORANGES   Orange sections may be arranged with nasturtium leaves and placed at base of stem glassware.

Gumdrop orange slice may be placed on the rim of the beverage glass together with a sprig of mint.

SPICES   Sprinkle cinnamon, mace, nutmeg, or other favorite spice over eggnog.

STRAWBERRIES   Float a whole strawberry with hull and stem on lemon or orange slice in a glass of strawberry punch.

Crush berries; sweeten to taste; pour over whipped cream floating on refreshing drink.

STRAWS   Serve colored straws or cellophane sippers with cold beverage to add color and a note of interest.

SUGAR Purchase colored or decorated cubes of sugar. Serve with hot or iced tea or any other beverage to which additional sugar may be added.

Orange cubes of sugar may be made by rubbing an ordinary lump of sugar over an unpeeled, slightly scraped orange and sprinkling with grated orange rind.

Breads

BACON Break grilled bacon into bits or curls. Place on top of unbaked muffins. They will become firmly attached during the baking.

CANDIES Sprinkle tiny decorative hard candies of various shapes, sizes, and colors over frosted sweet rolls or bread.

Press hard candies into sweet dough that has been shaped into coffeecake or rolls. Be sure to use candy that will not melt during baking.

COCONUT Scatter long or short shreds of coconut over frosted tea rings or rolls. White or tinted coconut may be used.

CORN MEAL Place a cardboard stencil over unbaked rolls, sprinkle corn meal over the design, then remove cardboard. Set rolls aside to rise; then bake.

EGGS   Use slightly beaten egg white, egg yolk, or whole egg. Brush over the top of biscuits or rolls just before baking.

FANCY FORMS   Crescents or Butter-horns   Separate dough into 12-ounce pieces. Roll each piece into a circle about ¼ inch thick. To obtain a perfect circle use a round pie or cake tin as a cutting guide. Brush with melted butter. Cut each round into 12 or 16 wedge-shaped pieces. Roll each wedge, starting at the broad end and rolling toward the point. Bend into crescent shape and place on greased baking sheet with point downward so it will not unroll. Brush with melted butter; let rise; bake.

Fans   Roll Danish pastry or other sweet dough ¼ inch thick; cut into 1-inch strips and brush with melted butter or shortening.  Stack five strips of dough and cut into 1-inch slices. Place the stacks with cut edges up in greased muffin tins. Let rise; bake.

Figure 8   Roll dough a little less than ¼ inch thick. Cut strips ½ inch wide and 8 inches long. Twist the strip and fasten the two ends together, making an oblong ring. Turn one end of the oblong over to form a figure 8. Let rise; bake.

Four-Pointed Star   Roll dough about ¼ inch thick. Cut 2-inch squares of dough. Then from each corner cut dough  almost to the center of the square. Bring every other point to the center and fasten the dough by turning the point under the end of the same section near center of star. Let rise; bake.

Knot Cut strips as for Figure 8. Tie a knot in center of dough. Place on greased baking sheet; let rise until light; bake.

Roses Cut 2-inch strips as for fan; arrange petal fashion in muffin tins. Be sure to overlap each petal like a rose in full bloom. Let rise; bake.

Yeast Cruller Roll dough a little less than ¼ inch thick. Cut ½ inch wide and long enough (about 8 inches) to wrap around a greased clothespin. Wrap so the edges barely touch. Place on greased baking sheet; let rise; bake. When baked, twist and pull out the clothespin. May be filled with jam or jelly.

FILLINGS FOR KOLACH AND OTHER SWEET DOUGH

Apricots

Cottage-cheese custard

Custard

Dates or dates and nut meats mixed.

Date paste, which is made by cooking 1 cup pitted dates with ½ cup sugar mixed with 1 tablespoon flour and a few grains of salt. Add ½ teaspoon lemon juice just before removing from stove. Cook until mixture is thick and smooth.

Prunes

FRANKFURTERS Arrange frankfurter slices in the form of a design on top of muffins just before baking.

FRUIT Candied Scatter chopped or minced candied orange, lemon, or grapefruit peel over quick coffeecake before baking or over frosting of yeast bread after baking.

Cut candied fruit in strips or in petals and arrange in design on frosted breads.

Form design with red or green cherry rings. Use with or without nut meat halves, as desired.

Large candied cherries may be cut to resemble poinsettias. Cut the cherry lengthwise into petals. Arrange petals on sweet bread or coffeecake to resemble a poinsettia. Use citron for leaves and stems.

Dried Place any one of the following fruits in rows or in any other design on coffeecake after the dough has risen and is just ready for the oven:

Apple slices or rings	*Peaches*
Apricots	*Prunes*
Currants	*Raisins*
Dates	

Pinwheels Roll a sweet dough about ¼ inch thick, brush with melted butter, then spread with a dried-fruit filling. To make the filling, chop apricots or prunes (which have been soaked slightly and drained thoroughly), dates, and nut meats, if desired. Scatter this filling over the sweet dough, roll like a jelly roll, and slice crosswise. Place cut side down on greased baking sheet; let rise; bake. The contrast in color produces a very pleasing effect.

Fresh Fresh fruit may be placed on the bottom of a greased baking dish, sprinkled with a little brown or white sugar, and dotted with butter. The dough is then placed on top and baked. Fresh fruit adapted to these uses are:

Apple slices or rings	*Cherries*
Berries of all kinds	*Rhubarb*

To serve, turn upside down on plate so that the fruit will be on top. The dough may also be placed in the baking dish first. The fruit is then prepared as above and placed on top of the dough before baking.

GINGER   Crystallized ginger may be cut in strips or chopped and sprinkled over dough before baking or scattered on top of frosted breads after baking. Using either method, the ginger may be arranged in a definite design.

ICING   Make confectioners' icing by combining 1 cup powdered confectioners' sugar with 3 tablespoons butter which has been melted in 3 tablespoons hot milk. Add ½ teaspoon vanilla.

Use the white frosting or tint with fruit or vegetable coloring. Spread over sweet breads or coffeecake.

Sprinkle frosting with chocolate shot, shredded coconut (white or tinted), or chopped or whole nut meats.

Place a cardboard stencil over the frosted bread while frosting is still soft, and sprinkle colored sugar over the pattern. Lift the cardboard and the sugar design will be formed on the frosting.

JAM, JELLY, MARMALADE   Place ½ teaspoon of jam, jelly, or marmalade on top of each muffin before baking.

Fill indentations on Moravian bread with jam, jelly, or marmalade.

Add 2–4 tablespoons jam, jelly, or marmalade to the frosting before spreading. The amount will vary, depending upon the thickness of ingredients and the consistency of frosting desired.

NUT MEATS   Any one of the following nut meats may be used on rolls, tea ring, or coffeecake:

*Almonds: whole, halves,
    shreds, or chopped.*
*Brazil Nuts: whole, shaved in
    slices, or chopped.*
Cashews: whole or chopped.
Filberts: whole or chopped.

*Peanuts: whole, halves, or
    chopped.*
Pecans: halves or chopped.
Pistachios: whole or chopped.
Walnuts: halves or chopped.

Arrange nut meats in a definite design or sprinkle on dough before baking, or on baked goods which have been spread with frosting.

SEEDS   Sprinkle caraway, poppy, or sesame seed over dough which has been formed into desired shapes and brushed with butter.

SPICES   Mix ½ cup sugar with 1 teaspoon cinnamon or ¼ teaspoon allspice, cloves, or mace. Sprinkle over coffeecake or rolls before baking.

SUGAR   Stir superfine sugar into ground nut meats; scatter over buttered unbaked tea ring or coffeecake.

With a sieve or flour sifter sprinkle superfine sugar over gingerbread.

Place cardboard stencil over frosted tea ring or rolls immediately after frosting. Sprinkle different-colored sugars through different parts of the design. Plan the arrangement so that you will have an attractive color combination.

For variation, mix together several different colored sugars and sprinkle on white frosting.

Cinnamon and sugar.
*Cinnamon, brown sugar, and
    raisins.*
*Cinnamon, brown sugar, and
    coconut.*

*Cinnamon, white or brown
    sugar, and chopped nut
    meats.*
*Coconut, honey, and nut
    meats.*

Cooked dried apricots, dates, figs, peaches, or prunes which have been sweetened to taste.

Cooked raisins and figs.

Rhubarb raisin topping. Combine 3 tablespoons melted fat, ⅓ cup sugar, 2 cups fresh rhubarb, ½ cup raisins. Mix well and place either in a well-greased pan with dough on top or spread over top of unbaked dough. A prettier effect is obtained if rhubarb mixture is baked under dough and turned upside down after baking.

Streusel topping made by combining ¼ cup flour, ½ cup sugar, ¼ cup butter, and 2 teaspoons cinnamon.

Cakes and Cookies

ANGELICA Cut stems and leaves from angelica and petals from cherries or dates. Arrange on cookies before baking or on frosted cookies or cakes.

Cut angelica into tiny dots. Arrange as border or design on sides or top of frosted cakes. May be used together with cherries or raisins cut in the same size. The frosting may be white or tinted.

ANIMAL COOKIES OR CRACKERS Arrange around edge of frosted cake either singly or in pairs. These are particularly effective on a circus party cake.

APRICOTS Dip edges of dried apricots in chocolate. When chocolate is set, arrange apricots in a design on frosted cake with cut side of the apricots down. Use dipping chocolate or blend 2 teaspoons of butter with 2 squares of unsweetened chocolate. Melt in double boiler.

CANDIES   Sprinkle tiny decorative candies over the top and sides of frosted cake.

Grind peppermint stick candy and scatter over the top and sides of frosted cake. Frosting may be white, tinted, or chocolate. For variation, place a cardboard stencil over the frosted cake and scatter ground peppermint candy over the design. Lift the cardboard without disturbing the design.

Use peppermint patties to form a design on a frosted cake. The patties may be used whole or cut with a sharp, thin knife into halves or smaller segments.

Gumdrops can be purchased in the shape of various objects, such as rabbits, eggs, hearts, shamrocks, according to the season. Arrange in a pattern on the cake.

CANDLES   Small colored candles inserted in tiny candleholders may be used to form the name or age of a person celebrating a birthday, or in any motif desired.

CHOCOLATE   Grate milk chocolate and sprinkle over a cardboard stencil placed over the top of a frosted cake. Lift cardboard carefully to obtain a perfect pattern. Grated chocolate is particularly effective on white or green-tinted frosting.

Melt semi-sweet chocolate in top of double boiler. Pour the melted chocolate from the tip of a teaspoon to form thin

circles on top of a white frosted cake. Draw the tip of a spoon or spatula through the chocolate lines from the outer edge toward the center. The outer circles may be left intact.

Swirl a soft frosting on top and sides of a cake. Insert chocolate tidbits or sprinkle chocolate shot over surface of frosting. Tidbits or chocolate morsels may be used to form a design on a white or tinted frosted cake.

COCONUT Sprinkle fresh shaved coconut or dried shredded coconut, either white or tinted, on the top and sides of a frosted cake.

COOKIES Form designs on a frosted cake with whole cookies, halves, or smaller segments. Attractive designs can be made on the sides as well as the top of a frosted cake.

Cut cookie dough in the shape of animals, flowers, or any other object to suit the occasion. Bake; place on frosted cake. Cookies may be frosted or left plain, as desired.

Make small fancy cookies with the various forms in the cookie press. Top with bits of cherry, dragées, tinted candied fruit peel, or colored sugar.

Animal Cookies Cut animals from your favorite rolled cookie dough and decorate with colored sugar, chocolate, candies, candied fruits, raisins, currants, fruit peel, nuts, coconut, and caraway seeds. Press decorating material in unbaked cookies or on baked cookies which have been frosted. Cookie cutters for the more common animals may be bought.

For the Card Party Hearts, clubs, diamonds, and spades may be cut from cookie dough. They may be decorated with nut meats, colored or white sugar before baking, or iced after baking and then sprinkled with colored sugar or tiny decorative candies.

Christmas Trees Cut cookies in the shape of trees, using a cookie cutter or a pattern cut from stiff cardboard. Sprinkle with sugar tinted green. Ornament with different colored candies; bake.

Christmas Wreaths Cut rolled cookie dough with a doughnut cutter. Sprinkle the cookies with green sugar; dot with tiny red candies; bake.

Crescents Cut dough with crescent-shaped cookie cutter or form a crescent with a round cutter by cutting a half circle then moving the cutter down about ½ inch from center of the arc and make another cut. Sprinkle with sugar and ornament with dragées. Blue sugar and silver dragées are very attractive.

Pinwheel Cookies Divide cookie dough into two equal parts. Add melted chocolate or pure-food coloring to one part and blend well. Roll the colored or chocolate dough in a rectangular shape about ⅛ inch thick on floured waxed paper. Roll light dough to same thickness and shape on another sheet of waxed paper. Place the light dough on top of the colored dough. Remove the waxed paper and roll as for a jelly roll. Place in refrigerator and chill until firm. Cut into ⅛-inch slices. Place on greased cookie sheet and bake.

Pumpkin Cookies Cookies may be cut with a large round cutter or with a pumpkin cutter. Place on a greased cookie sheet; bake. After baking, form leaves near the stem end with green icing forced through a decorating tube. For jack-o'-lanterns use a small slice of citron for the stem and fill in the eyes, mouth, and nose with melted chocolate or chocolate icing.

Variety Cutouts Roll cookie dough about ⅛ inch thick, and cut the cookies with a floured cookie cutter. The fancy cutters that may be used are stars at Christmas, hatchets for Washington's Birthday, shamrocks or pipes for St. Patrick's Day, and so on for every season or holiday of the year. If cutters are not available, cardboard patterns may be cut in various designs and used as a cutting guide.

FLOWERS **Candied Flowers** Asters, buttercups, nasturtiums, orange blossoms, pansies, rose petals, violets, or other suitable flowers. Use petals of fresh flowers. Press the petals softly in a cloth or paper towel to free them of all moisture. Weigh the petals. Take an equal weight of sugar, add a small amount of water, and boil to a sirup. Drop the petals into the sirup and boil until they look clear. Drain on a paper towel or fine wire rack. Dust petals with fine crystallized sugar. Place in a current of air in a sunny room, but not in direct sunlight. When sugar has been absorbed by the flowers, turn, and dust with more sugar. This process should be repeated until the surface of the petals is quite dry and covered with fine crystals of sugar. Arrange flowers on top and/or sides of cake singly, in clusters, or in a design.

Fresh Flowers Medium-sized or small blossoms may be used with their leaves on serving plates next to pieces of cake.

Painted Flowers Use pure fruit or vegetable colorings and a paintbrush especially reserved for foods. Paint flowers on the top and sides of a frosted cake. The frosting should be somewhat hardened before applying the colorings.

FROSTING **White** Cover entire cake with a white frosting, then place a cardboard stencil over top and sprinkle sweet grated chocolate over pattern. Remove cardboard gently to obtain a perfect design.

Cover cake with white or tinted frosting. Shave Brazil nuts into lengthwise slices and arrange in petal fashion to form flowers on top of cake. Use half a candied cherry for the center of each flower and green citron for the leaves. The flowers may be arranged in clusters or singly to form a border around the top of the cake.

Shave Brazil nuts into lengthwise slices and sprinkle over the top and sides of frosted cake to cover the cake completely.

Scatter tinted coconut over white frosting or white coconut over tinted frosting. Place a candied cherry with green citron leaves in the center of the cake.

Place a cardboard stencil over the frosted cake. Sprinkle shredded coconut over the pattern and lift cardboard carefully to produce a perfect design.

Sprinkle green-tinted coconut over a white frosted cake. Arrange tiny bluebirds on top of cake either in groups of two or three or to form a border around top of cake. Plastic bluebirds may be purchased in novelty or five-and-ten-cent stores.

Mark off the top of a round cake into 12 or 16 wedges, depending on the size of the cake. Make three small batches of different-colored frostings. Spread every third wedge in a different color and continue the frosting down the side of the cake. The different colors will appear as  broad stripes on the side of the cake. A few of the many combinations that may be used are:

Dark brown (*chocolate*),
   light brown (*maple or butterscotch*), *and green*
   (*mint*)
Yellow (*lemon*), *orange*
   (*orange*), *and green* (*lime*)

Pink (*strawberry*), *green*
   (*mint*), *and white*
Red (*cherry*), *yellow*
   (*lemon*), *and green*
   (*mint*)

Cover entire cake with chocolate frosting. Decorate with white or green frosting which is forced through pastry tube.

Use a paper pastry tube or a decorating set to form pictures, designs, or lettering on frosted cakes. Make a soft frosting, divide it into several small batches, and tint each batch in a color necessary to form the picture or design.

FRUITS Candied apricots, prunes, pineapple, cherries, lemon, orange, or grapefruit peel, in natural color or tinted, may be used for decorating cakes. Cut in the shape of petals to form flowers or in geometric figures to form signs.

Dried fruit may be used in similar ways.

Fresh fruit, such as berries, cherries, or other small fruit may be used in clusters on top of freshly frosted cake or next to individual servings on the dessert plates.

GINGERBREAD HOUSE
To make the gingerbread dough, mix and sift together 3 cups flour (scant), 2½ teaspoons baking powder, ½ teaspoon salt, 1 teaspoon ginger, and ¼ teaspoon cinnamon. Beat 1 egg; add ⅓ cup sugar, ⅔ cup molasses, and ⅓ cup melted shortening. Combine with dry ingredients and knead slightly to form smooth dough. Chill. Cut pattern pieces from lightweight cardboard. The pattern shown is ⅓ actual size. Roll out a piece of dough to a rectangle ⅓ inch thick and a little larger than pattern to be followed. Then carefully lift the dough and place on a greased baking sheet. Place the pattern pieces on the dough and cut around the edges with a sharp knife.

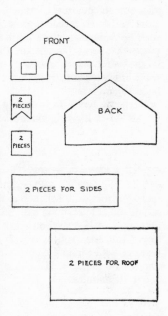

Remove the remnants of dough, leaving the house sections, and bake at 375° F. for 10 to 12 minutes. Follow the same procedure for all pieces of the pattern. Allow to cool thoroughly.

To Decorate and Put House To-
gether Decorate the front, the door,
and the chimney pieces with red cinnamon drops attached with sugar
sirup. To make the sirup, cook ½ cup
sugar, ¼ cup water, and a few grains of cream of tartar to
300° F., or until a small amount is brittle when dropped in a
glass of cold water. Remove from fire and place over hot
water so sirup will not harden too fast. With a small, clean
paintbrush spread a little sirup where decorations are to go
and quickly put the candies in place. Put the two sides and
front and back pieces together by brushing edges with sirup,
then hold them in place until the sirup hardens. Put the two
pieces that form the roof and the four chimney pieces together
in the same manner. Attach the door. To put snow on the
roof, brush it with sirup, then sprinkle generously with granulated sugar.

**Keep the house in a cool, dry place so that the sirup will
not soften or the gingerbread become soft.**

GINGERBREAD MEN Dissolve ½ cup shortening in ¼
cup boiling water. Add ½ cup brown sugar and ½ cup
molasses; mix well. Mix and sift 3 cups all-purpose flour, 1 teaspoon soda, 1 teaspoon salt, ½ teaspoon ginger, ½ teaspoon
nutmeg, and ⅛ teaspoon allspice and combine with first mixture. Chill, then roll. Cut with gingerbread-man cutter. Make
features with candied cherries, raisins, or colored candies. Use
dragées for buttons. Bake in a moderate oven (375° F.) for
about 10 minutes.

HOLLY Place fresh sprigs of holly at the base of a cake.

Paint a holly design on the top and sides of cake.

Cut holly berries from candied cherries and leaves from
citron. Arrange on a frosted cake.

HONEY   Top honey cakes with sections of honeycomb.

JELLIES OR JAMS   Beat jelly or jam until smooth enough to pass through a decorating tube. Form concentric circles equidistant on a frosted cake. After the circles have been formed, draw the tip of a pointed knife or spatula through each circle toward the center. Repeat this process, beginning from the outer circle, at intervals of every 1½ to 2 inches.

Drop a bit of jelly around the edge of a frosted cake to form a border. Use no more than ⅛ teaspoon of jelly or jam and space each drop about 1 inch apart.

LEAVES   Frosted mint leaves   To frost, dip leaves in egg white beaten to a froth, shake off excess egg white, then dip in powdered sugar. Repeat until all the egg white is absorbed and a white surface is obtained. Place on tinted or chocolate frosted cake.

Arrange fresh mint leaves on the top, sides, or base of a cake.

Leaves from bushes, flowers, or trees in season may be placed at base of a cake. Use singly or in clusters.

MARSHMALLOWS   Cut white or tinted marshmallows into tiny pieces and form circles or other designs on the top and sides of a cake. Whole marshmallows may be placed at the base of a cake, alternating white and pink or white and green.

Dip part of a marshmallow in melted chocolate; let stand until firm; place in design on cake.

With pure fruit or vegetable dye paint faces on marshmallows. Place on cake with the faces turned out. Make caps with pieces of pressed figs and place on the marshmallow heads.

MARZIPAN   Form scrolls, flags, flowers, or other objects to suit the occasion. Marzipan is pliable and can be purchased in many colors.

MISTLETOE   Use fresh mistletoe at the base of a cake or on a serving plate next to an individual serving of cake.

NUT CRUNCH   Crumble pecan or other nut crunch on a cutting board with a rolling pin and scatter on the top and sides of a frosted cake.

NUT MEATS   Form a design with pecan, walnut, or peanut halves on top of a frosted cake.

Scatter chopped pistachio or other nut meats over the design of a cardboard stencil which has been placed on the top of a frosted cake or cookies. Lift cardboard gently to obtain a perfect pattern.

Form flowers on the top and sides of a cake or on the top of unbaked or baked and frosted cookies with blanched toasted almonds or whole pistachio nut meats.

Dip a third of each blanched toasted almond into melted chocolate. Use in this way, or sprinkle chopped pistachio nut meats over melted chocolate, allow to harden, then arrange on cake or cookies.

SPICES   Sprinkle cinnamon, mace, nutmeg, or any desired spice sparingly over a frosted cake, or over a cardboard stencil placed over a frosted cake.

TOPPINGS   Crush graham crackers, mix with a little sugar and cinnamon if desired, then sprinkle over a cardboard stencil which has been placed over a frosted cake. Remove the cardboard gently so as not to disturb the design. The outlines of girls, flowers, fruit, trees, houses, or any object may be cut in medium stiff cardboard which has been shaped to fit the top of a cake. The design should be clean cut with no ragged edges.

WHIPPING CREAM Swirl either white or tinted whipped cream on the top and sides of a cake or force through a pastry tube to form rosettes or other designs on the top and sides of a cake.

MISCELLANEOUS SUGGESTIONS

1. Cut cake into squares and cover with slices of brick ice cream. Top with whipped-cream rosettes and sprinkle with chopped pistachio nuts.

2. Hollow out cupcakes. Line with jam or jelly and fill with ice cream. Arrange tinted whipped cream roses and leaves on the rim of each cupcake.

3. Cover slices of angel-food cake with vanilla ice cream. Sprinkle with crushed fruit and top with a sprig of mint.

4. Remove the center of a spongecake so that only a 1-inch wall remains. Fill this "basket" with peach ice cream which has been blended with whipped cream. Place chilled peach slices on rim of the basket.

5. Calla Lilies Beat 3 eggs until thick and lemon-colored, add ¾ cup sugar and 1 cup cake flour mixed with 1 teaspoon baking powder. Add vanilla. Drop by spoonfuls on a greased cookie sheet about 3 inches apart. Bake in a 400° F. oven until done—about 5 minutes. Remove at once and roll like a cone. Place on a rack with folded side down; let cool. Serve filled with angel parfait. Insert a strip of candied orange peel or gumdrop for the stamen. Tint whipped cream green and pipe around edges. Place a sprig of mint at the small end of each cone.

6. Caramel Baskets   Combine 1½ cups brown sugar, 2 teaspoons corn sirup, ½ cup milk, and ¼ cup butter or margarine. Cook, stirring occasionally, to soft-ball stage (238–240° F.). Pour the hot sirup over shredded wheat in a buttered mixing bowl. Mix well. Pack in well-buttered muffin pans, shaping to form cups. Chill until firm. To serve, unmold and fill the center with peach slices and berries. Top with whipped cream.

For variation, fill basket with chilled custard and top with fresh berries or fill with berries and fresh-fruit ice cream.

7. Angel-Food Dainties   Make your favorite angel-food cake; cut a slice from top of cake. Hollow out the center of the cake, leaving at least a 1-inch wall of cake on the outside. Mix 6 tablespoons cocoa, 6 tablespoons sugar, and ⅛ teaspoon salt with 3 cups of whipping cream, then chill. Whip the cocoa-cream mixture until stiff. To part of the whipped-cream mixture add ½ cup sliced blanched and toasted almonds. Fill the center of cake with this mixture. If desired, sprinkle sliced toasted almonds over the cake. Chill before serving.

Mint Whipped-cream Filling   Flavor 1½ cups whipping cream with a drop or two of oil of peppermint, and tint green, if desired. Fill hollowed angel-food cake with the cream mixture which has been sweetened to taste. Replace the top of the cake and cover with Cocoa Whipped Cream.

Pineapple-Cherry Bavarian Cream   Soak 1 tablespoon gelatin in 1 tablespoon cold water and stir into ⅓ cup boiling pineapple juice until dissolved. Do not boil the gelatin. Cool until as thick as molasses. Add 1¼ cups whipping cream and whip the mixture until stiff. Add 2 tablespoons sugar, ¼ cup shredded drained pineapple, and ¼ cup cut maraschino cherries. Fill the angel-food cake with the Pineapple-Cherry Bavarian Cream and put in refrigerator to set.

Raspberry Filling   Dissolve 1 package raspberry gelatin in 1½ cups boiling water. Place in refrigerator until slightly congealed, then whip with a rotary beater until thick and smooth.

Fold in 1 pint of heavy cream, whipped, 1 pound of frozen or 3 cups of fresh raspberries, and small squares of angel-food cake; fill a hollowed-out angel food cake. The section of cake that is cut out to make an angel-food "basket" may be separated into small pieces and used in the filling. Place in refrigerator until set. Top each individual serving with fresh raspberries.

Raspberry-Coconut Filling Cut a slice from the top of an angel cake, hollow out. Be careful not to break outer wall. Crumble the cake which has been removed and mix with ½ cup shredded coconut, 1 cup canned raspberries, drained, ½ teaspoon vanilla, 2 tablespoons sugar, and 1 cup heavy cream, whipped. Fill the cake with the fruit mixture and replace the top. Chill for 3 hours. Spread with 1 cup heavy cream, whipped and sweetened to taste; sprinkle with ½ cup coconut and top with fresh raspberries, if available.

8. Checkerboard Cake Cream 9 tablespoons shortening and add 1½ cups sugar gradually while creaming. Sift 3 cups cake flour; add 3 teaspoons baking powder and ½ teaspoon salt; sift again. Add flour mixture alter- 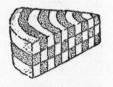 nately with 1 cup milk and 1½ tea- spoons vanilla. Fold in the stiffly beaten whites of 4 large eggs. To one third of this batter add a chocolate mixture by blend- ing 2 tablespoons sugar, 4 tablespoons hot water, and 2 squares melted unsweetened chocolate. Add ⅓ teaspoon soda and stir until thick. Use three layer pans. In 2 pans arrange a ring of the white-cake mix about 1 inch wide around edge of pan; then a chocolate ring 1 inch wide, and so on, until five rings have been formed. In the third pan start with a chocolate ring near rim of pan and continue alternating colors until five rings have been formed. If available, use special checkerboard pans. Bake in a 350° F. oven for about 20 to 25 minutes. Put the layer containing the chocolate outer ring between the other two layers. Spread each layer with frosting, and frost top and sides of cake.

9. Place a lace doily over the top of an unfrosted cake. Sprinkle powdered sugar over the doily, then remove the doily gently so as not to disturb the lace design on the cake.

10. Easter Lamb To make the cake lamb mold, cream 5 tablespoons butter and 1 cup sugar. Sift cake flour before measuring, then measure 2½ cups plus 2 tablespoons, resift it with 2½ teaspoons tartrate or phosphate-  type baking powder or 2 teaspoons double-action (sulfate-phosphate) baking powder. Measure ⅔ cup milk and add 1 teaspoon vanilla to it. Sift about a third of the flour mixture into the creamed butter and sugar, add about a third of the milk mixture, and beat batter until blended. Repeat this step, adding a third of the milk and the flour mixture until all the milk and flour mixture has been added and beaten until blended. Beat 2 large egg whites and ¼ teaspoon salt until stiff (but not dry) and fold them into the batter. Grease a lamb mold with melted fat or oil. Fill the deeper part of the mold (front of the lamb) with the batter, spreading it evenly. Do not forget to spread it into the ears. Preheat the oven to 350° F. Place the mold on a cake tin and bake for 50 minutes to 1 hour. Test the cake, and when it is done remove the upper half of the mold. Allow the cake to cool before removing it from the mold. If a piece of the lamb's body breaks off, use a toothpick to hold it in place. Ice the lamb with white icing and cover it with grated coconut. Use two raisins for the eyes and a bit of cherry for the mouth. Place the lamb on a bed of green leaves or grass. If available, place small flowers on the grass and hang a bell on a ribbon around its neck. Note: A spiced-cake recipe may be used in place of the white cake, if desired.

Desserts

ANGELICA Chop angelica and sprinkle over the dessert.

Cut a stalk of angelica into lengthwise slices, then cut each lengthwise slice into thin strips to form the staff for music notes of a definite melody. Other shapes may also be cut from these slices and arranged on individual or general desserts.

APPLES Cut firm, tasty apples in julienne strips. Make cinnamon sirup by cooking 1½ cups sugar, 1 tablespoon corn sirup, 1 cup of water, and a 2-inch piece of stick cinnamon for about 10 minutes. Simmer apple strips in the sirup until tender. Tint the sirup any pastel color desired with pure fruit coloring and allow the apple strips to stand in this colored solution overnight. Arrange strips fence fashion near the base of the dessert, or crisscross on top of the dessert.

APPLESAUCE Tint applesauce green, then form into nests

on top of individual desserts or at the base of a molded dessert served on a large plate. Fill with whole nut meats, Bing cherries, blackberries, blueberries, ground cherries, raspberries, strawberries, or other available small fruit.

BANANAS   Slice bananas and arrange as a border around the bottom of a dessert glass or on top of a large dessert in alternating rows with other fruit.

Dip one half of a banana slice in pineapple juice and the other half in melted chocolate. Allow the chocolate to harden, then arrange the slices in a design on the dessert.

Flute the bananas by drawing the tines of a fork down the outer surface of a whole banana. Cut slices diagonally, then dip in pineapple or other fruit juice. Stand upright in petal fashion on top of the dessert, inserting just enough of the banana slice to stabilize it.

BERRIES   Form borders or other designs with fresh whole berries. Use singly or in clusters with or without mint leaves or natural leaves.

Slice strawberries and arrange artistically on dessert or pour the crushed fruit over the dessert.

CANDIES   Place cinnamon hearts or drops in a design on any light-colored dessert.

Crush stick candy of any chosen color and flavor; sprinkle over white dessert.

Cut peppermint patties in half or in smaller segments and arrange in a conventional design.

Decorative candies: Scatter over the surface or arrange in a definite pattern tiny, hard, smooth surface or rough lacy candies. These candies come in a number of colors, flavors, and shapes. The tiny star-shaped candies are particularly attractive.

CHERRIES   Arrange a cluster of red, white, or black cherries with the leaves at the base of stemware containing the dessert. Two or three cherries may be fixed on the rim of the glass or on the top or side of the dessert.

Pit cherries. Beginning from open end of the cherry cut petals by cutting down to but not through the center at the other end. Spread out on the dessert. Arrange singly, with or without leaves and stems, or in groups to form bouquets.

Chop red or black cherries and arrange in design.

CHESTNUTS   Purchase candied or brandied chestnuts. Slice or chop the chestnuts and decorate desserts of a contrasting color.

CHOCOLATE   Drip melted chocolate in a pattern over dessert.

Scatter shot or place morsels of chocolate in definite pattern.

Pour chocolate sauce over dessert and top with chopped nut meats, cherry, or colorful hard candies.

CITRON   To decorate desserts with citron designs, cut light-colored citron in the shape of various objects. Color by allowing the cut citron to stand overnight in a thin sirup solution colored with fruit or vegetable coloring. Stems and leaves may be cut from deep green citron.

Chop citron; scatter over dessert or form a definite design by sprinkling generously over a cardboard stencil which has been placed over the dessert. Remove cardboard carefully and a perfect design will be formed.

COCONUT   Grate or shave fresh coconut and sprinkle over dessert.

Toast coconut and scatter over dessert. Use either long or short shreds.

Scatter short shreds of white or tinted coconut over a cardboard stencil. Remove cardboard carefully so as not to disturb the design.

COLORING   Using fruit or vegetable coloring, tint part of a light-colored pudding, then gently mix the light and the colored portions to give a marbled effect. For variation arrange in layers in glass stemware.

Meringues or whipped-cream toppings may be tinted to give a two-tone effect.

Paint designs on white or light molded desserts with a paintbrush and fruit or vegetable coloring.

COOKIES   Place tiny whole cookies, halves, or smaller segments of a large cookie in a design to suit some special occasion. Cookies are used most effectively on soft or molded desserts.

CREAM PUFFS OR ECLAIRS   Make tiny cream puffs, using about ¾ or 1 level tablespoon of dough. Bake and let cool. Fill with custard or whipped-cream filling and top with white or tinted whipped-cream rosettes. Arrange around any dessert served on a torte plate.

CRANBERRIES   Insert different lengths of small sticks (the size of toothpicks or thinner) in fresh cranberries. Then group all together with mint or other suitable leaves to form a bouquet. Place a small bouquet at the base of a glass or other stemware or arrange groups of the cranberry bouquets at intervals on a torte plate.

Cook cranberries gently until tender in a sugar sirup so that their shape will be retained. Place in tiny meringue rosettes and use as border at the base of a dessert. Serve on a large plate.

Cut cranberry jelly about ½ inch thick, then cut into special shapes with a cookie cutter or other fancy cutter. Serve on dessert. For example, serve cranberry bunnies on top of tapioca pudding; sailboats on vanilla junket; little chickens on rice fluff or other light dessert.

Use thick cranberry sauce or softened cranberry jelly (jelly that has been beaten with a fork) in alternate layers with a white fluffy mixture made by combining a beaten egg white with 1 cup of heavy cream, whipped, 1 teaspoon flavoring, and 2 tablespoons sugar.

DATES Stuff dried dates with nut meats, then cut into slices or use whole in an artistic arrangement.

Chop dates or cut in strips. Fashion in the shape of flowers or other designs. Use orange rind for the center of the flowers.

DESSERT BUNNY Use a large scoop of ice cream for the head and strips of marshmallow for the ears. Place the scoop of ice cream on a serving plate. Tint the insides of the marshmallow ears with pink vegetable dye, then fasten the ears to the ice cream with toothpicks. Form the eyes and nose with bits of raisins and the mouth with a piece of cherry. The whiskers can be made with long shreds of coconut or shredded wheat. Force whipped cream through a pastry tube to form the collar. Serve immediately, or place in freezing compartment of refrigerator until ready to serve.

DESSERT CLOWNS Prepare gelatin according to directions on the package. Chill until slightly sirupy. Pour half of mixture into four to six cone-shaped sherbet glasses. Place in refrigerator. Chill remaining gelatin in bowl until almost firm. Beat with a rotary beater until fluffy and thick. Pour over plain gelatin in sherbet  glasses. Chill until firm. Place three cookie halves on each individual plate to form a circle. Unmold gelatin on top of cookies. Whip cream until stiff. With a pastry tube, decorate with whipped cream to represent a clown's face, hat, and ruffled collar.

Place a large scoop of ice cream on a serving plate and top with an ice-cream cone for the hat. Form eyes, nose, and mouth with raisins and cherries. Force tinted whipped cream through a pastry tube to form the ruffled collar.

FIGS Chop or cut figs in strips and form geometric designs on desserts.

FLOWERS Candied. See Index.

Fresh flowers. See Index.

FRUIT Cut brandied or candied fruit in various shapes. Arrange in design on the dessert.

Place a small segment of crystallized grapes on top of dessert or at base of glass stemware containing dessert. A small cluster may be placed on the rim of a glass or several clusters may be arranged at intervals on a torte plate next to a molded dessert. To crystallize grapes, select 1 pound of red or purple grapes, wash and dry well, then cut into small clusters. Combine ½ cup water and 1 cup sugar and boil 5 minutes. Dip each bunch of grapes separately into the sirup, allow excess sirup to drain off, and sprinkle grapes immediately with coarse granulated sugar. Place on a platter and allow sirup to harden. Grapes will crystallize more rapidly if placed in the refrigerator.

Arrange whole or sliced fresh fruit with or without leaves on top of dessert or in groups around the dessert.

Make a sauce with fruit juice, tint color desired, and pour over dessert.

Chop or cut dried fruit into strips and use to form ships, flags, or other objects to suit the occasion.

FRUIT ICE   Scoop tiny balls of fruit ice or sherbet and serve on top of diced fruit, melon balls, or whole berries, with or without mint leaves. Be sure that the ice has a dominant color or one in contrast to fruit used.

GELATIN   Mold flavored gelatin in a flat pan to a depth of ½ to 1 inch. Cut in the shape of animals, flowers, or any object desired, and arrange on the top or sides of a dessert.

Shred flavored gelatin, place different colors in a frappé glass, alternating colors in layers either flat or at an angle.

To make attractive designs in gelatin molds, choose substantial, clean-cut pieces of fruit, such as peach or pear slices, orange or grapefruit sections, grape halves, melon balls, strawberry halves, or slices of stuffed prunes. Vegetables could be used in salads in the same way. Turn slightly thickened gelatin mix into a mold to make a thin layer about ¼ inch thick. Place fruit in the pattern desired. Chill until firm. If the design is not perfectly set, place another thin layer of gelatin over fruit and chill until set, then fill mold with the remaining gelatin. Additional fruit may be inserted around sides. In arranging fruit in a design, remember that when gelatin is unmolded, the form will be upside down.

More elaborate designs may be arranged on top of any mold, using whole small fruits or carefully cut pieces. A simple arrangement in each corner or in the center of a mold or as a border is always attractive. More elaborate wheels, flowers with "petals," chains, diamonds, and circles are lovely if carefully done.

GINGER   Cut preserved ginger in shapes desired and arrange on dessert.

GRAPENUTS   Sprinkle on top of white or tinted topping of desserts.

HOLLY   Use berries, leaves, or sprigs at base of stem glassware or around plum pudding.

HONEY   Drip strained honey in any appropriate design over the topping on a dessert.

JELLY OR JAM   Place a spoonful on top of meringue in individual servings.

JELLY ROLL   Arrange slices of jelly roll on the bottom and sides of a round mold. Fill the center with a tasty, fluffy gelatin mixture, such as strawberry charlotte. Top with jelly-roll slices, then chill until firm. Cut mold in wedges to serve. This makes a very attractive dessert.

KUMQUATS Slice fruit and arrange in overlapping slices at the base of a dessert on a torte plate, or place a few slices on top of a pudding.

LEMONS Cut each slice in fancy shapes. Place on rim of glass or on greens at base of glass.

Sprinkle grated rind over dessert.

Pour lemon sauce over dessert; top with whipped cream or grated lemon rind.

MACAROON OR CAKE CRUMBS Sprinkle crumbs over entire surface of a dessert, or over a cardboard stencil. For directions how to use cardboard stencil, see Helpful Hints in section on general directions.

MARRON GLACÉ European chestnuts which have been steamed or boiled and glazed. Use as a topping for ice cream or other dessert.

MARSHMALLOWS Cut white or tinted marshmallows in halves or pieces and use to form rabbits.

Place whole marshmallows on certain desserts, put under flame, and puff just before serving.

MELONS Scoop balls from watermelon, honeydew, or

muskmelon with a French ball cutter. Arrange in nests or in rows, groups, or circles at base of dessert. Intermingle with watercress or mint leaves.

Cut small slices of melon and insert in a dessert at intervals. Top with berries.

Cut melon in lengthwise wedges. At one end of each wedge place a cluster of grapes with leaves or berries and mint leaves.

Serve a scoop of ice cream in the center of a crescent-shaped piece of honeydew melon or in a half muskmelon. Place whole berries on melon around ice cream. Attach a sprig of mint. Grapes may be cut in half lengthwise, seeded, and used in place of berries. Place on the melon with the cut side down.

MERINGUE   Use white or tinted meringue on dessert. Form designs by forcing through a pastry tube; place in a 375° F. oven until set. Remove; serve plain, or fix cherries, dragées, or other colorful decoration in each design.

Poach meringue in hot water until firm; remove; drain; place in serving dish. Pour soft custard over top of poached meringue. Meringue will float. A bit of jelly, jam, or marmalade placed here and there on meringue will add color and flavor.

Sprinkle shredded coconut over meringue before baking.

NUT MEATS   Almonds   Blanch, shred, and scatter over the surface of a pudding before baking. Or toast whole blanched almonds and use singly or in groups to form a design.

Brazil Nuts   Shave or chop and sprinkle over dessert.

Cashews   Use whole or chopped.

Peanuts   Remove brown membrane, use whole, halves, or chopped.

Pistachios   Form geometric or conventional designs with whole or chopped pistachio nut meats.

Walnuts   Form a center design or a border with halves. Chopped walnuts may be sprinkled over a cardboard stencil. To obtain a perfect pattern remove cardboard carefully.

ORANGES   Arrange three orange slices in a circle, overlapping each other, and place a maraschino or candied cherry in the center of each slice. The stems of 2 or 3 mint leaves may be placed under each cherry.

Insert orange sections in the sides of a molded dessert or around the edge of a dessert served in a deep dish.

Sprinkle grated orange rind over dessert.

Cut candied orange peel, tinted or in natural color, in shape of objects, flowers, or geometric figures. Arrange in design that will harmonize with shape of container.

Dip candied orange peel in melted chocolate. Let stand until hard, and arrange in design.

PEANUT BRITTLE OR PECAN CRUNCH   Chop or break in small pieces; scatter over or place in center of individual servings of dessert.

PEARS   Tint cooked pears a delicate green, pink, or yellow by allowing them to stand overnight in a colored sirup made by adding fruit or vegetable coloring to the pear sirup. Arrange two or three groups of whole pears, pear halves, or slices on greens surrounding a dessert served on a large plate.

PERSIMMONS   Cut a persimmon in sections. Arrange around a large buffet dessert, either alone or combined with other fruit.

PINEAPPLES Cut fresh pineapple in cubes and arrange border fashion at the base of molded dessert. Scatter whole berries or chopped mint over pineapple.

Stand canned whole pineapple slices at intervals in a fruit border surrounding a watermelon or honeydew melon bowl which has been filled with mixed fresh fruit. Galax leaves may be used under the melon bowl on top of a serving tray.

Make or buy candied pineapple. Use in natural color or tinted. Decorate a dessert with wedges or halves of pineapple slices with or without candied cherries.

PINE NEEDLES Select choice twigs of pine needles, clean thoroughly, and place at each end of a long oval tray on which a plum pudding is served. The pudding may be topped with an alcohol flame made by inserting a small special glass container in the top of the pudding filled with alcohol that is lighted just before pudding is served.

PRUNES Stuff cooked pitted prunes with marshmallows, nut meats, or candied fruit. Place on top of individual dessert or arrange in groups on top or at the base of large general dessert.

Form flowers from prunes which have been cut in shape of petals.

RAISINS Scatter whole raisins, dried or puffed by steaming, over dessert, or use in design. To steam raisins soak 20 minutes in enough water to cover. Drain. Place in a perforated container, such as a colander, over hot water, and steam 20 minutes.

SAUCES A few of the popular sauces which may be used on desserts are berry, chocolate, custard, foamy, hard, Hawaiian, honey, jelly, lemon, maple, marshmallow, mint, nutmeg, orange, tutti-frutti, and yellow. Each will give a different decorative touch to puddings or other desserts.

Hard sauce may be formed in various shapes or molds, such as lambs, little men or women, wigwams, or other seasonal objects.

STRAWBERRIES Place whole strawberries, with or without hulls, on top or at the base of a dessert. Berries may be sliced and used in a design at bottom or sides of a glass bowl or to form design on top of dessert.

Crush berries, add sugar to taste, and place in a serving dish, alternating the layers of berries with layers of a light fluffy dessert. Top with whole berries.

Scatter whole or crushed berries over a whipped-cream or meringue dessert topping.

TANGERINES Separate tangerines into sections and arrange in design on or around pudding. Sections of tangerines may be marinated in brandy for a few hours before using, then drain well and dry on a paper towel if necessary before placing sections on the dessert.

WHIPPING CREAM Swirl white or tinted whipped cream or force through a decorating tube over the dessert. If desired, top with chopped nut meats, cherries, chocolate shot, or fruit strips.

Scoop out the center of a cupcake, fill with a ball of ice cream, and decorate the rim of the cupcake with whipped cream to form a fluted border. Force pink-tinted whipped cream through a decorating tube to form pink rosettes at intervals on the whipped-cream border.

Fish

ANCHOVIES Wrap anchovy fillets around stuffed olives; arrange in groups around fish and intersperse with parsley.

ASPARAGUS Insert three or four asparagus tips in a green pepper or pimento ring. Place four bundles on a fish platter, two at each end. Arrange at an angle parallel to the fish.

ASPIC Mold colored, well-seasoned aspic in a fancy mold or in a flat pan about ½ inch thick and cut into fancy shapes. Place in lemon or lime cups or in a bed of garnishing greens around fish. To make the lemon or lime cups, cut the fruit in half lengthwise and remove pulp carefully. Edges may be plain or scalloped. Well-seasoned fish may be molded into the aspic.

BACON Before baking, top fish with slices of bacon. During baking the bacon will curl to a certain extent. Place the grilled bacon curls around the fish.

BEETS   Cook small or medium-sized beets, rub off skin and remove tops. Scoop out center of beets and fill with a well-seasoned vegetable of contrasting color. Arrange filled beets in groups or place at intervals around fish.

Cook beets and slice while hot. Arrange in groups of three overlapping slices and alternate with cooked Brussels sprouts to form a border around fish.

Fill small parboiled onion cups with chopped cooked beets.

BREAD   Cut bread in fancy shapes, such as hearts, clubs, diamonds, et cetera. Deep-fat fry and arrange as a garnish around fish.

Scoop out a 2- or 3-inch square of bread to make a bread foundation. Fill with creamed fish and top with a bit of parsley.

Make bread boats from long diamond-shaped pieces of bread cut about 2½ inches thick. Fill with creamed fish, sprinkle grated cheese on rim of boat, and return to oven to toast bread and melt cheese. Insert a carrot cut in the shape of a sail in front of the boat.

CARROTS   Cut off the large end of a carrot, about 1½ inches deep. Parboil, then scoop out center portion to form a cup. Fill with fish sauce or fish dressing, then arrange as many cups as needed to make an attractive border around the fish. Carrot cups may also be filled with buttered peas instead of a sauce.

Score carrots with a fluting knife; slice, cook, and then arrange in design over fish.

Cut raw or cooked carrots in julienne strips and arrange as border around baked fish. Insert parsley here and there.

With a French ball cutter scoop balls from large parboiled carrots. Place in nests of mashed potatoes or shredded greens, such as cooked spinach or Swiss chard.

CHARD Shred chard, mix with a slightly beaten egg, season to taste, then bake in custard cups. Remove the chard by inverting the custard cups. Arrange the mounds of chard as a border or in groups around fish. Top each mound with a slice of hard-cooked egg sprinkled with paprika or garnished with a star or other shape cut from pimiento.

CHEESE Mold tinted cream cheese in shape of birds' eggs. Place in nests of shredded greens; arrange nests around cooked fish on large platter.

Grate cheese and sprinkle over baked fish. The heat of the fish should melt the cheese. If it does not, put in oven long enough to melt cheese.

Pour cheese sauce over fish and sprinkle with paprika.

COLESLAW Prepare green or red coleslaw with sweet-sour dressing. Fill cooked onion or turnip cups with slaw, then arrange between servings of fish fillets.

Use coleslaw to make nests; fill with tiny fish balls made from fish-croquette mixture.

CUCUMBERS Cut off the large end of a cucumber about 2 inches deep. Do not peel. Scoop out pulp, then cut peel in 5 petals and shape each petal like that of a water lily. Place in ice water to open. Insert carrot slice for center of lily. Place among greens next to fish on a large platter.

Cut a 1¾-inch section from the end of a large peeled or un-peeled cucumber. Scoop out pulp. Fill with olive-tomato sauce. Make a carrot spoon by carving a raw carrot into the shape of a spoon.

Make a cucumber basket by cutting peeled or unpeeled cucumbers into 2-inch pieces from end of cucumber. Cut the edge in notches. Scoop out the center portion. To make the handle, cut a slice from the large part of a second cucumber, then cut out the center to form a ring that will fit over the top of the basket. Two thirds of the cucum-  ber ring is usually needed to form the handle. Fasten the handle in place with toothpicks.

Score an unpeeled cucumber with a fluting knife. Cut slices and arrange in greens around fish.

Cucumber Twists   Cut a large cucumber into thin slices, then cut each slice through up to the center. Pull the ends thus made in opposite directions to form a curl and hold in place with a toothpick. Chill, then remove toothpick and place among greens around fish.

Slice a cucumber into thin lengthwise slices. Roll, then fasten with toothpicks and chill in ice water. Remove the tooth-picks and arrange among greens on a fish platter. Fringe edges before rolling if desired.

EGGS   Cut a hard-cooked egg in halves, quarters, or slices. Top with chopped parsley, paprika, or pimiento cut in narrow strips or shapes of objects and place around salmon loaf. Bits of truffle or grated cheese may be sprinkled over fish loaf and toasted just before serving.

Cut perpendicular gashes in a hard-cooked egg and insert cucumber slices in the gashes formed.

Mince the white and yolk of a hard-cooked egg, separately or together, and sprinkle over creamed fish.

Top beet slices with slices of hard-cooked eggs and arrange around fish loaf.

ENDIVE Curly endive (chicory) is particularly effective used as a border on fish platters because of its feathery texture and variegated color, which ranges from yellow green to dark green.

HORSE-RADISH Fill small cucumber or beet cups with ground, well-seasoned horse-radish. Serve on fish platter.

LEMONS Stud rind of lemon slice with whole cloves, or form cross on top of lemon slice with inserted whole cloves.

Cut a lemon slice about ½ inch thick, then use whole or cut in wedges. Cut gash in rind in middle of each wedge. Insert a scored cucumber slice. If whole slice of lemon is used, insert scored cucumber slices in gashes made in rind ¾ to 1 inch apart. The outer edge of cucumber may be dipped in paprika.

Cut lemons in half crosswise or lengthwise and remove pulp. Stuff with fish salad, cut in wedges, and arrange in design on fish platter.

Serve fish sauce in lemon cups. To make lemon cups, cut a lemon in half lengthwise and remove pulp carefully.

Cut lemons in sections, top pointed edge with strips of pimiento or whole cloves.

LOBSTER   Arrange lobster claws, feelers, or corals around lobster on large platter.

MUSHROOMS   Sauté mushroom caps, fill with browned minced onion or top with piece of pimiento; arrange in a row on top of baked fish. Sliced mushrooms may be used in the same way.

OLIVES   Chop ripe, green, or stuffed olives, and sprinkle on top of fish sauce.

Cut stuffed olives in half crosswise; stand on edge as dividing lines between servings of fish fillet.

Arrange ripe, green, or stuffed olives in nests of shredded lettuce or watercress surrounding fish.

ONIONS   Cut onion slices and separate into rings. Arrange a row of rings over large fish before baking, overlapping the rings to form lacy effect.

Arrange small parboiled onions in bed of greens as border around baked fish.

PAPRIKA   Use brilliant red variety of paprika. Sprinkle over fish or dip edges of greens into paprika before arranging on fish platter.

PARSLEY   Chop parsley; scatter over cooked fish or sauce.

Arrange sprigs of parsley generously on fish dishes.

PIMIENTOS   Cut pimientos into shape of stars and place or top of cone-shaped croquettes.

Scatter bits of pimiento with green pepper or chopped parsley over creamed fish.

Arrange strips of pimiento, cut in different lengths, over fish cakes.

PINEAPPLES   Sauté pineapple slices or finger strips. Stand a 2-inch section of whole cooked carrot in center of pineapple ring; or insert pineapple finger through cooked carrot ring. Arrange at intervals around fish platter. Top carrot in pineapple ring with a star or other shape cut from green pepper.

Sprinkle chopped parsley and paprika in alternate wedges on slice of pineapple.

Dip outer edge of pineapple slice or wedge in paprika. Place small French-fried fish balls in center of pineapple ring.

PEPPERS   Cut a green or red pepper in rings, strips, or cups. Fill the cups with fish sauce. Alternate or interlace red and green rings or strips around or on fish.

POTATOES   Scoop potato balls with a French ball cutter. Parboil, butter, sprinkle with chopped parsley, and arrange in shredded carrot nests. Carrots may be cooked or left raw.

Make lattice potatoes by cutting the potato with a fluting cutter. Make one crosswise cut, then turn the potato and make the second cut at right angles to the first. A perfect latticed slice will be obtained if the slice is thin enough to obtain an open lattice effect. Deep-fat fry and arrange around fish.

Cut potatoes in julienne strips, deep-fat fry, and arrange in mounds around fish.

Force hot mashed potatoes through a pastry tube to make rosettes or other design around baked fish.

Mold cold mashed potatoes into the shape of apples, sprinkle paprika on one side, insert a bit of parsley at stem end and a whole clove at blossom end. Heat the potato apples in oven before garnishing fish platter.

RADISHES   Form bouquet with radish roses, tulips (For directions see radishes in Appetizer section.), and daisies and intermingle with watercress on platter. To make radish daisies, cut a crosswise slice through center of large radish, then cut petals freehand with a sharp paring knife, or cut around a daisy cardboard pattern which has been placed on radish slice. When making radish flowers, leave enough stem on each radish so that they can be fastened together with thread.

RICE   Mold well-seasoned rice in croquettes of various shapes, dip in slightly beaten egg and fine cracker crumbs, then deep-fat fry. Top with a bit of cranberry-orange relish.

SAUCES   Use a sauce that will lend color as well as flavor to the fish: egg, hollandaise, oyster, shrimp, Spanish, or tartar.

SHALLOTS   Chop shallots and use in place of onions.

SHELLS   Serve clam, crab meat, or other sea food in clam shells. They will make an attractive dish for an otherwise drab-looking fish food.

SHRIMP   Clean shrimp, dip in fritter batter, deep-fat fry, then arrange in groups around baked fish.

SMELTS Deep-fat fry smelts, place on a slice of Bermuda onion or tomato, and use as garnish on fish platter.

SPINACH Shred cooked spinach, shape into nests, and fill with cooked, well-seasoned carrot balls.

TOAST POINTS Cut ½-inch slice of bread into small triangles. Sauté and stand upright in border around fish.

TOMATOES Place small plum tomatoes in groups in a bed of greens on platter of fish fillets.

Broil tomato slices, top with chopped chives, arrange at ends of fish platter. Raw tomato slices may be used topped with grated cheese.

Cut a slice from the top of each of several small tomatoes. Scoop out the center and stuff with well-seasoned rice, bread, or meat filling. Grill, then arrange on platter with cooked and buttered broccoli.

TROUTLETS Carve cold canned or cooked salmon croquette mixture in shape of trout. Roll in slightly beaten egg and fine cracker crumbs. Deep-fat  fry. Serve hot on platter and garnish with watercress. Use little pink or red candy peppermint drops for eyes of fish. These fish should be small in order to serve as a border around large baked fish.

Meat

ALMONDS Sprinkle shredded almonds over tomato sauce on meat loaf.

APPLES Cinnamon Apples Cook sugar and water together for about 5 minutes, using ¾ cup sugar for every ½ cup water. Tint red with cinnamon candies or red fruit coloring. If the fruit coloring is used, add a piece of stick cinnamon for flavor. Add apple rings, and simmer gently in sirup until tender but firm. Do not crowd apples. Remove from sirup, drain, arrange around meat in groups of 3, then fill rings with mint or other flavored jelly, or with pitted prunes.

Glazed Apples Use 4 apples. Wipe, remove cores and a portion of the skin, then peel upper half of apples and place close together in a saucepan with the peeled side down. Add ½ cup boiling water, cover tightly, and steam until tender but firm. Transfer to baking dish, peeled side up, sprinkle with ½ to ¾ cup sugar, and place in broiling oven until sugar is dissolved, basting with ¼ cup of liquid in which apples were steamed.

Variations   Add fruit coloring and flavoring to the water before steaming apples.

Chill glazed baked apples, fill centers with raisins, sliced dates, or cooked prunes.

Beat ½ cup whipping cream until stiff; gradually add 1 to 2 tablespoons honey while beating. Add ¼ cup chopped walnuts or other nut meats and a few grains of salt. Fill centers of glazed apples with this mixture.

Top apples with red jelly just before serving, or cover apples with melted jelly after they have been removed from the oven. Allow jelly to congeal. If necessary, repeat process until apple has a clear, thick glaze.

When baked apples are almost tender, put a marshmallow in the center of each and return to the oven or broiler to toast and brown.

Use juice of one orange; add enough water to make ½ cup liquid. Cover apples with grated orange rind. Follow directions for glazed apples. When ready to broil, fill centers with broken pecan nut meats.

Apple Cups   Use red-skinned apples. Trace parallel lines about ½ to 1 inch wide to form a band around the middle of an apple, then take a sharp knife and cut diagonal lines within this band, cutting through to the center of the apple first in one direction then in the opposite direction, to form triangles. When you have  cut completely around the apple, it will separate into two parts, both having scalloped edges. Scoop out pulp; remove core. Cook in cinnamon sirup until tender but firm. Drain; fill with buttered peas, mincemeat, sweet potatoes, or other suitable vegetable.

Applesauce Serve either hot or cold applesauce, in natural color or tinted, on toast points or in eclair shells.

Apple Fritters Arrange tiny apple fritters around meat, either as a border or in groups.

Crabapples Place tiny hot spiced crabapples in a row or other design on top of meat loaf or arrange at side in groups. Cold crabapples may be intermingled with greens.

Sauté apple rings or sections and serve with pork.

APRICOTS Pan-broil apricot halves in their own sirup; serve with a hot spiced prune in center of apricot. Use in groups of 3 at end of meat platter or space evenly around platter.

ASPARAGUS Insert three or four asparagus tips in pimiento or carrot ring. Serve hot in design on meat platter.

Stand three or four asparagus tips upright in firm red or yellow tomatoes which have been scooped out just enough to admit stalks. Heat before arranging on platter.

Roll partially cooked asparagus tips in a slice of minced ham or other cold cuts; fasten with a toothpick; baste with butter, and broil until meat begins to crisp. Arrange around meat loaf.

ASPIC Cut colored aspic jelly into cubes or other shapes. Fill small tomato, carrot, pepper, cooked onion, or beet cups.

BACON Top meat loaf with crisscross strips of bacon. When baked, place slices of stuffed olives at points where bacon strips cross.

BANANAS Glaze whole small bananas or sections of large bananas by broiling and basting with brown sugar sirup. To make sirup combine ¾ cup brown sugar and ½ cup water. Arrange bananas in fan shape next to meat.

Wrap bacon around bananas, sauté or bake, and arrange on meat platter according to shape of roast.

BEETS Fill beet cups with tiny meat balls, turnip balls, or Brussels sprouts.

Scoop balls from cooked beets with a French ball cutter and use separately or in combination with other vegetable balls in bed of greens on meat platter. Heat vegetable balls before placing in greens.

BISCUIT TOPPING Cut baking-powder biscuit dough or other meat topping in shape of rabbits, chickens, shamrocks, or other suitable objects; or cut in geometric designs. Space far enough apart on meat dish so that objects will remain separated when baking.

BRUSSELS SPROUTS Arrange cooked Brussels sprouts in groups at ends of platter. Alternate with young whole cooked carrots.

CABBAGE Shred cabbage, marinate in sweet-sour dressing, and drain. Arrange as border around meat or form into mounds or nests. Top mounds with strips of pimiento and/or green pepper; fill nests with hot meat balls.

CARROTS Grill young whole carrots, fasten a small piece of carrot leaf or parsley at stem end, and use as garnish for meat platter.

Cut whole carrots into lattice slices. Use a 2-inch end of carrot; make a crosswise cut with a fluting knife, then turn the carrot and make a second cut at right angles to the first. Continue turning the carrot a fourth turn for each slice. Each slice should have an open lattice effect. Cook the lattice slices gently or use raw on meat platter.

See Fish Section for other suggestions.

CAULIFLOWER   Separate a head of cauliflower into florets. Use cooked florets with hot meat dishes; top with grated cheese or paprika. Raw florets make an excellent garnish for cold cuts or meat salads. Arrange on meat tray in attractive groups.

CELERY   Use fringed celery or leaves on hot or cold meat dishes. To fringe celery, cut both ends of a 3-inch piece of celery into ¼-inch strips. Leave a ¾-inch band of celery uncut in the center of stalk. Place in ice water to curl.

CHUTNEY   Serve chutney or other highly spiced relish in tiny lettuce cups or in cooked carrot, beet, or onion cups.

COCONUT   Sprinkle coconut on top of mashed sweet potatoes in scalloped orange cups. Use 1 cup for each person and arrange around roast duck.

CORN   Fill mashed-potato nests with whole-kernel corn. Form the nests by forcing the mashed potatoes through a pastry tube.

Arrange tiny hot corn fritters around roast.

CRANBERRIES   Place cranberry bouquets in greens on meat platter. See directions for making bouquets in appetizer section. Use cranberries on toothpicks.

Serve cranberry-orange relish in tiny timbale cases. To make relish use 4 cups raw cranberries and the pulp and thin outer skin of two oranges. Grate or pare this skin with a sharp knife and discard the white membrane. Grind cranberries, orange pulp, and peel in food grinder. Add 2 cups sugar and mix well. Let stand at least 24 hours before using.

CROQUETTES   Use leftovers, such as rice, meat, or vegetables. Form into small cones or other shapes, such as balls, animals, or nests, then deep-fat fry and arrange on meat platter. Fill nests with cubed cooked carrots or beets.

CUCUMBERS   Serve cucumber relish in vegetable cups or tiny patty shells.

Place a teaspoon of chutney on top of scored unpeeled cucumber slices. Arrange around meat on platter.

CURRANTS   Garnish meat platter with bunches of fresh currants with or without leaves. Wash and dry well before using.

Serve currant jelly in lemon or lime cups. To make the cups, cut the fruit in half lengthwise and remove pulp carefully.

EGGS   Place colored Easter eggs around base of baked ham among sprigs of watercress or parsley.

Shell hard-cooked eggs and paint with fruit or vegetable coloring. Or allow eggs to stand in colored pickling solution overnight. Use same as above.

Place a shelled colored egg in a canned peach half. Alternate varied colored eggs in groups of three around roast or baked ham.

FIGS   Alternate spiced figs with orange slices that have been topped with pitted prunes. To spice figs, wash 1 pound of pulled figs, soak 1 hour in cold water, and drain, then add 2 cups vinegar, 3 cups sugar, 2 tablespoons cloves, and ½ ounce stick cinnamon. Cook slowly until figs are tender, adding water if sirup gets too thick. Spiced figs are unusual and delicious.

FLOWERS **Vegetable Flowers** *Brown-*
eyed Susan From stem end of carrot cut 3 thin 1½-inch lengthwise slices. Fashion each slice into 3 petals; overlap slices at base and insert a ripe olive in the center.
If desired, curl carrot slices before using by placing in ice water for an hour or so.

California Poppy Cut curved slices
from large end of carrot to resemble petals of a California poppy. Overlap petals at base and fasten with a toothpick. Use sprig of parsley for foliage and a piece of truffle or other dark material for the center of the flower.

Calla Lily Cut a white turnip in very thin crosswise slices and roll to form calla lily. Use 2 slices for each lily if the turnip is small. In-
sert a carrot strip for the stamen and use parsley, mint, or watercress for foliage. Fasten with a toothpick. To make an Easter lily, cut each overlapping slice of turnip into 3 petal shapes and finish in the same way as the calla lily.

Carrot Jonquil Use a 2- or 3-inch piece of carrot; cut five petals rather thin near the surface with a rounding blade if available. Round off carrot petals. Fasten petals at base. Place in ice water to open.

Cucumber Rose Use a 2-inch piece of cucumber. Cut petals to form at least two layers near the surface. Chill in ice water. Use any available greens for foliage.

Daisy Cut slices from either turnip or rutabaga about ¹⁄₁₆ inch thick. Make a cardboard pattern of a daisy, place on vegetable slice, and trace outline of flower with the point of a knife. Remove pattern and cut around outline with a sharp knife. Use a slice of carrot, candied or fresh orange peel, a piece of truffle, or ripe olive for the center of the flower.

Jonquil Make a cardboard pattern according to the size of the flower desired. Peel rutabaga and cut in very thin slices. Use a 3-inch biscuit cutter to cut slices of rutabaga into circles. Trace jonquil  pattern on one circle with a pencil or pointed knife, then cut out flower. In the center of the design cut a small round hole about ¼ inch in diameter. Through this hole slip a folded piece of rutabaga made from one third of the second 3-inch slice, letting it extend 1 inch through the opening. This forms the center of the flower. Cut the petals toward the center, molding them so that they curl in natural shape. Chill flowers in ice water to keep them crisp. Before serving, tint lightly with yellow vegetable coloring by placing flowers in ice water to which liquid vegetable coloring has been added.

Narcissus Make a cardboard pattern of a narcissus. Cut ¼-inch slices of white turnips. Dip edges of the tiny center cylinder in paprika and fasten in place with a piece of toothpick. For greens, use spinach leaves or mint leaves. For directions in making cylinder see Jonquil.

Tomato Rose Hold a firm, medium-sized tomato in the left hand. Beginning from blossom end of fruit, remove a thin peeling with a sharp knife, cutting in wavy lines about 1 inch wide. Continue around the tomato to stem end, being careful not to tear the peel. If stem has  been left on the tomato, it will be easy to hold. Wind peel, let rose rest on stem, then fasten with a toothpick. In winding, keep the bottom part of the rose a little tighter than the upper part. The petals will open gracefully, just like a rose. Use rose leaves or any other greens available. Roses may be made from red, yellow, and white tomatoes. The edges of the white tomato rose may be dipped into pink or red fruit or vegetable coloring. White tomatoes, of course, are scarce and may not always be available.

Bouquets of Flowers Cut flowers from slices of carrots, turnips, or rutabagas with fancy cutters. Combine with whole raw cranberries fastened to toothpicks. Place on bed of greens. It is easier to arrange the carrot, turnip, and rutabaga flowers if they are fastened to toothpicks.

Fruit Flowers *Shasta Daisy* Use a 3-inch round of fresh or candied orange peel. Trace a circle about ¾ inch in diameter in the center of the peel, then cut ¼ inch wide petals up to this circle. Place a slice of date, a piece of prune, or a large seeded raisin in the center of the daisy.

Grapefruit or Orange Rose Cut peel from fruit in deep scallops, starting at stem end and continuing around the fruit. Do not break the peel. Rewind, keeping the base firm; fasten with toothpicks. Arrange in bed of watercress or mint leaves. Edges and white membrane may be colored by allowing the peel to stand in water tinted with pure fruit or vegetable coloring.

Tulip Cut petals from orange rind which has been carefully removed in sections from whole orange. Cut cucumber peel into strips for stem and leaves. Candied orange rind may be used instead of the fresh peel.

Water Lily A water lily may be made by following directions for tulips except that petals are cut shorter.

FORCEMEAT Use any favorite recipe and form balls or other shapes. If poultry, meat, and other ingredients are minced fine enough, the mixture can be forced through a pastry tube to form rosettes and other designs on meat loaf or dressing served in orange cups. Bake about 20 minutes before serving.

GELATIN Prepare any tasty gelatin and color to suit taste, occasion, and color theme. Mold or cut into desired shapes. (See directions for aspic in appetizer section.)

Turn gelatin mold onto a pineapple or orange slice and arrange on meat platter.

To form a flower design on a jellied meat loaf, use slices of stuffed olives and stems and leaves cut from green pepper. Pour a layer of gelatin mix about ¼ inch deep in a loaf pan and allow to stand until firm. Arrange the olive slices and green-pepper stems and leaves in a flower design on top of the gelatin. Pour another layer of gelatin mix ¼ inch deep over the design. Allow to congeal, then fill the rest of the mold with cold baked meat loaf. To decorate the sides, dip the pieces of olive and green pepper in the gelatin mixture and fix in place when the layer of meat is high enough to stabilize them. When meat loaf is unmolded, the design will be fastened to the top and sides of the jellied meat loaf.

GRAPES Simmer seedless grapes or raisins, dark or white, in wine for about 10 minutes. Remove grapes or raisins and thicken wine slightly with cornstarch; cook thoroughly. Add fruit, and cook until raisins or grapes are well puffed and flavored. Pour over baked ham or other meats, as desired.

HOLLY Arrange sprigs of fresh holly around base of baked ham or roast. A sprig may also be placed on top of baked ham.

JELLY Place apple, currant, mint, or other jelly in tiny lettuce cups, on toast points, in small colored paper cups, in fruit or vegetable cups, or on top of an orange slice. The color of the jelly should harmonize with the color of its container. Arrange around lamb or other roast.

KUMQUATS Parboil and remove slice from top of each kumquat. Do not peel. Scoop out a little of the pulp and fill the cavity with sugar. Place the kumquats upright and close together in a shallow baking pan and pour a little pineapple juice over them. Bake in a 375° F. oven for 15 minutes.

LEMONS AND LIMES Baskets Mark the outline of the basket with the point of a sharp knife, then cut away the two upper quarters, leaving a strip about ⅓ inch wide to form the handle of the basket. Scoop out the rest of the pulp  carefully so that the handle will remain intact. Scallop the edge of the basket. Fill with relish or other condiment.

Cut a lemon or lime in half lengthwise or crosswise, remove pulp, and serve plain or with scalloped edges. Fill with horseradish, tartar or cranberry sauce, or jelly. Place two or four of the cups on the meat platter.

Place a cardboard stencil over a lemon slice, then sprinkle paprika, chopped parsley or chives over the stencil design. Remove cardboard carefully. If desired, top lemon slice with a mint cherry, mint spray, or grated orange rind instead of paprika and chopped chives.

MEAT Pinwheel Use large bologna slices. Cut each slice into 4 sections, making each cut to within ½ inch of the center of the slice, then fold every other corner to the center, and fasten the points to the center with a piece of toothpick and half of a stuffed olive.

MISTLETOE   Use in the same way as holly. See directions in this section.

MUSHROOMS   Place pan-broiled mushroom caps in design on top of meat loaf just before serving, or pour sauce containing chopped mushrooms over top of meat.

Place broiled mushroom caps on the top of dressing or vegetables served in vegetable cups.

Fill mushroom caps with carrots and peas.

OLIVES   Garnish meats with a cluster of ripe, green, or stuffed olives in a bed of greens.

Insert toothpicks in any one of all three kinds of olives to form bouquets, or arrange olives in design on baked ham.

Form a design on a roast or ham with sliced stuffed olives.

ONIONS   **Raw**   Cut onion in slices; top each slice with a mushroom cap, truffle, or sliced olive. If desired, the onion slices may be tinted by placing in water to which vegetable coloring has been added.

Cooked   Dip raw onion rings in timbale batter, deep-fat fry, then arrange on top of meat or around a roast.

Cook a large onion, then remove enough pulp from the center so that three asparagus tips can be inserted. Use short asparagus tips and place upright in the onion cup. For variation, candles may be made by using small boiled onions. Remove enough onion with an apple corer so that 1 asparagus tip can be inserted. Attach a strip of green pepper on the side of the onion for a handle. Arrange the candles at intervals around roast on platter.

Fill cooked onion cups with hot baked beans.

ORANGES Baskets or Cups. See directions for making lemon baskets in this section. Fill with cubed cranberry jelly or sauce or other relish.

Form nests by filling orange cups with mashed potatoes forced through a pastry tube. Place buttered peas in nests. Sweet potatoes may be used in the same way. For variation place marshmallows in center of potato-orange cup. Heat just before serving to puff marshmallow.

Fill a pear half with mint jelly and a maraschino cherry with stem and place on an orange slice. Arrange a sprig of mint near the stem end of the pear.

Grill orange slices, then top with a red or green maraschino cherry.

Fill beet, turnip, or carrot cups with orange jelly. To make the orange jelly, soften 2 tablespoons unflavored gelatin in ½ cup cold water; add 1½ cups boiling water, ¾ cup sugar, 1 cup orange juice, ¼ cup vinegar, and the grated rind of 1 orange. Stir well until sugar has dissolved, strain through cheesecloth, and pour into a flat pan to congeal. Cut into squares, cubes, or fancy shapes.

Stuffed oranges. Boil seedless whole oranges until quite tender, cool, then cut in half. Scoop out some of the pulp and fill with a mixture of chopped nuts, crystallized ginger, and candied cherries. If necessary, add a little sugar to sweeten the mixture. Place the filled orange halves in a shallow pan and pour sirup over them. To make the sirup, boil 2 cups sugar, ⅓ cup white corn sirup, and 1 cup water to 234° F. Place in a hot oven and heat for 20 to 30 minutes. Baste with sirup mixture. Top each orange half with a maraschino cherry and arrange around roast duck or turkey.

PEACHES Fill peach halves with well-seasoned chutney, jam, or jelly.

Broil peach halves in their own sirup.

Remove the pit from whole spiced peach. Cut pulp into the shape of water-lily petals. Arrange on platter and place pitted prune in center of each flower.

Cut pitted spiced whole peach into petals. Beginning at one end cut down to, but not through, center at the other end. Flatten out to spread petals. Place a round of candied orange peel or slice of date in center of flower.

Stud spiced whole peaches with whole cloves and/or almonds cut in julienne strips. Arrange three pieces of fruit at each end of a large platter.

Fill the cavity of a peach half with a white or tinted marshmallow. Just before serving, heat enough to puff marshmallow. For variation, surround marshmallow with raisins.

PEARS Use small whole or medium-sized canned pear halves. Tint green, pink, or other desired color by soaking in the sirup to which pure fruit coloring has been added, then broil until well heated through. While broiling baste with sirup made with 4 tablespoons brown sugar, 1 tablespoon butter, and ½ cup water.

Pear Airplane Use a canned whole pear or large pear half. Insert blanched whole almonds at the blossom end of the pear to represent the propeller. Cut a banana in half lengthwise and dip in pineapple or other fruit juice, then  cut a small opening in both sides of the pear and insert the banana pieces to form the wings of the airplane. Cut two slices of red-skinned apple, dip in fruit juice, and insert at right angles over the small end of the pear to form the tail of the plane. Place on a bed of curly endive. This makes an attractive garnish for a cold-meat platter.

Place alternating strips of green and red pepper or pimento crosswise or lengthwise on spiced pear.

Crush corn flakes, then roll whole or half canned pears in the crumbs. Bake until heated through and arrange on meat platter rounded side up.

With paintbrush and fruit coloring, paint a small whole canned pear as it appears in natural color. Insert a whole clove at blossom end and a crabapple stem together with a few mint leaves at stem end. Arrange in groups of 3 on meat platter.

PEPPERS Cut green or red pepper in various shapes, such as stars, flowers, or seasonal designs. Place on meat or on light-colored vegetables surrounding meat.

Shred pepper, use separately or combine with shredded carrots or beets, and arrange in small mounds surrounding meat.

Cut red or green peppers in half, then remove membrane and seeds. Fill with cabbage slaw or creamed whole-kernel corn.

Parboil green pepper cases, fill with hot diced beets, cooked onions, or meat balls. Pepper cases may be filled with any meat or vegetable combination and baked. Arrange as many around meat as there are people to be served.

PICKLES Sweet-sour cucumber pickles, dill or mustard pickles, or spiced melon pickles may be served in lemon, lime, or orange baskets or in fruit or vegetable cups or on tiny lettuce leaves. See directions for making lemon baskets in this section.

Chop pickles and serve on toast points arranged around meat.

PIMIENTOS Firecrackers Wrap a wide strip of pimiento around a cocktail frankfurter to resemble a firecracker. Insert a small strip of green pepper for the fuse. Grill. Serve next to ham slices on the Fourth of July.

Cut pimiento into strips or fancy shapes. Use on meats to add a note of color.

PINEAPPLES Sauté rings of pineapple in a small amount of fat, or a combination of fat, pineapple juice, and brown sugar. Top each ring with a prune which has been stuffed with an orange section, or a canned apricot half filled with a marshmallow. If marshmallows are used, heat garnish to toast the marshmallows just before serving.

Stud outer edge of pineapple ring with whole cloves. Broil; fill center with cranberry mold.

Roll edge of pineapple ring in paprika or chopped parsley. Place mushroom cap in center of ring.

PLUMS Spiced Green-gage Plums Drain sirup from a No. 2½ can (3½ cups) of green-gage plums. Heat sirup and suspend a small cloth bag containing 12 cloves, 1-inch stick cinnamon, ¼ teaspoon whole allspice in the sirup. Boil for 5 minutes. Pour over the fruit and let stand several hours. Drain. Tint pears pink with pure fruit coloring. Arrange on platter with roast duck or goose.

Prune Plum Cut prune plum in half lengthwise and stuff with marshmallow; or cut plum in sections and arrange in the form of a flower on a roast or on the platter next to a roast.

Cut prune plum in half lengthwise, arrange in groups of 3 around meat. This is especially effective when meat is served on a white platter.

POTATOES Flavor mashed sweet potatoes with sherry wine. Place in mounds around meat and top with chopped peanuts.

Bake potatoes. Scoop out the inside and prepare as whipped potatoes. Make nests in the potato shells by forcing the whipped potatoes through pastry tube. Fill with buttered peas, cubed carrots, whole-kernel corn, or sautéed link pork sausage. Meat balls about the size of marbles may also be served in these potato nests. Heat before serving.

Deep-fat fry lattice potatoes and serve in mounds around roast. For making lattice potatoes, see directions for potatoes in fish section.

Shred raw potatoes, dry well, and place in lower wire basket. Make enough shreds to line the basket completely and to form a sturdy nest. Insert top basket and fry in deep fat. Remove wire basket gently so as not to break the nest. Fill with vegetable cubes or balls and place as many nests around meat as there are people to be served. Meat balls or Easter eggs may also be served in these nests.

PRUNES Serve spiced prunes in beds of greens or on tiny skewers around meat. To spice prunes combine 2 cups prune juice with 1-inch piece of stick cinnamon and ¼ teaspoon mace. Boil for 5 minutes, remove from heat, pour over prunes, and let stand several hours. Drain; stuff the prunes with finely chopped cooked meat, preserved watermelon pickle, marshmallows, candied orange peel, or orange sections.

RADISHES Place radish roses, tulips, jonquils, or daisies on meat platter at points of interest. See directions for radishes in appetizer and fish sections.

RICE Form molds of rice cooked with prunes, figs, dates, or raisins. Top each mold with any one of these fruits whole, if not too large, or cut in shape of petals.

SAUCES Serve brown, lemon, orange, or tomato-olive sauce in gravy boat. Top the sauce with one of its major ingredients: fasten a lemon slice on edge of gravy boat containing lemon sauce, or tomato-olive sauce with slices or stuffed olives, et cetera.

SQUASH Cut acorn squash in half and remove seeds and membrane. Bake, then fill with buttered peas and top with strip of grilled bacon. Arrange around roast.

TIMBALE CASES Make timbale cases ½ to ¾ inch high. Cut sautéed Polish link sausage in 1½-inch pieces, place one in the center of each timbale case, and surround with buttered peas. For variation, place a mushroom cap in center of timbale case and surround with peas or tiny carrot balls.

TOMATOES Fill a white or green vegetable cup with tomato-pear chutney. To make chutney, mix together 1 pound chopped tomatoes, 1 pound chopped pears, 1 chopped pepper, 1 chopped onion, ⅛ teaspoon cayenne, ½ teaspoon mustard, ½ teaspoon ginger, 1 teaspoon salt, ½ cup vinegar, and 1 cup white sugar or 1¼ cups brown sugar. Boil slowly for 1 hour, stirring occasionally. Add 1 small can of chopped pimiento and boil 5 minutes longer. Pack into sterilized jars; seal at once. Use as needed.

Slice tomatoes and top each slice with a rosette made by forcing piquant butter through a pastry tube. For variation, grate American cheese or processed cheese and mold into the shape of animals, vegetables, or other objects. Place in the center of each tomato slice.

Top broiled tomato slices with steamed unbleached raisins.

Broil tomato cups filled with vegetable or meat mixture.

TRUFFLES Cut truffles in strips or fancy shapes, top orange slices or light-colored vegetables surrounding meat.

TURNIPS   Parboil turnips, then cut slice from one end and scoop out the pulp. Edges may be scalloped or left plain. Dip edges in paprika which has been sprinkled on a plate or other flat surface. Fill the hot turnip cups with buttered peas, whole-kernel corn, diced beets, or other diced, colorful vegetable.

Slices of raw turnip may be cut into many shapes. Dip edges in paprika or chopped parsley.

VEGETABLE AND FRUIT COMBINATIONS   Cut peppers lengthwise to form cases and fill with rice in tomato sauce. Form a border of the stuffed pepper cases around meat.

Combine raw turnip balls and red cabbage relish. Serve in lettuce cups on meat platter.

Surround a standing rolled roast with any of the following:

Pineapple slices dipped in chopped parsley and topped with cranberry mold.

Peach halves filled with fresh gooseberries.

Rice molds topped with a border of cubed carrots and buttered peas in the center.

Thick tomato slices topped with mushroom caps.

Place meat balls in center of blue plate or platter and arrange sautéed onion slices around edge. Top with whole-kernel corn, then scatter green pepper and pimiento strips over surface of corn.

Mold ham loaf in round shape. Place peach halves, round side up, on outer rim of loaf, overlapping peach halves slightly. Fill center with cooked parsleyed onions.

Pies and Pastry

ANIMAL COOKIES OR CRACKERS Cut gashes in the pastry used for the top crust of a blackberry pie before baking, so that there will be one, two, or three openings in each wedge. Just before serving the pie, place small blackbird cookies in the gashes.

Lay or stand animal crackers on a custard or chiffon pie.

CANDIES Scatter colorful decorative candies over meringue or whipped-cream topping.

Arrange dragées in a design on each wedge of a pie before baking.

Hard candy hearts or gumdrop candies in many shapes may be used to form designs, such as hearts, clubs, diamonds, flowers, or other objects on the surface of a pie.

CHERRIES, CURRANTS, AND GOOSEBERRIES Arrange a cluster of fruit with leaves next to each pie wedge on serving plate. If the whole pie is served at the table, a cluster of fruit may top the center of a two-crust pie or be arranged artistically on the rim of a glass pie dish.

CHEESE Mold processed cheese into a small apple and sprinkle one side of the "apple" with paprika. Insert a whole clove at the blossom end and a crabapple stem at the stem end. Serve on apple pie. The cheese may also be molded into the shape of a pumpkin. Mark ridges on the pumpkin with the dull edge of a knife and insert a whole clove in the stem end. Serve on pumpkin pie.

GRAPES Swirl meringue or whipped cream on top of the pie so that there will be a swirl on each wedge. Place 3 whole grapes in each swirl.

Place each wedge of pie on a serving plate and arrange a small cluster of grapes with mint leaves over the crust.

MERINGUE Press meringue through pastry tube to form rosettes, dividing lines, or other designs on pie.

Top pie with white meringue and cover with white or tinted coconut.

Scatter chopped or shaved nut meats over meringue.

Top meringue with berries or slices of fruit.

NUT MEATS Press nut-meat halves in top piecrust before baking.

Form designs with nut-meat halves on custard pie after baking.

PASTRY CUTOUTS Cut chickens, rabbits, hatchets, shamrocks, or other objects out of unbaked piecrust; place a cutout on each pie wedge, then bake.

Trace a unit of cherries with leaves on the piecrust, then cut out the design with a sharp knife. Place a cherry unit on each serving of an open-faced cherry pie before baking.

Trace then cut three large maple leaves from piecrust. Place on top of fruit pie, then bake. After baking, place in the center a few pieces of the fruit that was used in the pie—whole berries or other small fruit or a few slices of larger fruit.

Cut oak leaves and an acorn out of piecrust. Mark the veins on the leaves with the tip of a knife. Place one unit on each serving, then bake. For variation, leaves may be cut out of ¼-inch slices of American cheese. Trace the  leaves on paper or cardboard, cut out, and use as patterns. Mold the acorn and acorn cap from processed cheese and attach the cap to the acorn. Dip the cap in chopped nut meats or nutmeg. Place the cheese acorns and oak leaves on individual servings of apple pie or other 2-crust pie just before serving.

Trace then cut strawberry leaves from piecrust. Sprinkle leaves with green sugar and bake. Top each serving of cream pie with strawberry leaves and a fresh whole strawberry with or without hull.

Roll pastry about ⅓ inch thick; cut into the shape of a star. Make a hole in the center of each star large enough to insert a candy candleholder. Bake. Just before serving place the candleholder with candle inserted on top of pie wedge.

PINEAPPLE Arrange pineapple wedges in a flower design, with a half or a whole cherry for the center, on top of a baked pineapple custard pie or in the design stenciled on top crust of a two-crust pineapple pie before baking.

SPICES Sprinkle cinnamon, nutmeg, mace, or any other suitable spice over custard pies, or over whipped cream on pie.

SWEETENED CRUMB MIXTURE Prepare cookie or cake crumb mixture by rolling dried cookies or cake. Scatter over meringue or whipped-cream-topped pies, or sprinkle over design in cardboard stencil. Hold stencil slightly above the pie topping to prevent its touching the soft whipped cream or meringue.

WHIPPED CREAM Top entire pie with white or tinted whipped cream. To tint whipped cream add fruit or vegetable coloring to the cream before beating.

Top whipped cream with jelly or any of the following fruits: bananas, prunes, dates, figs, plums, or cranberries.

Scatter grated sweet chocolate, chocolate shot, chopped nut meats, or white or tinted coconut over whipped cream.

Using pieces of fruit, form flower designs on whipped cream in individual servings.

Force whipped cream through pastry tube to form design on pie or pastry. Top with chopped pistachio nut meats.

Arrange nut-meat halves in a design on top of whipped cream.

Salads

A BEAUTIFUL GARNISH can be lost on a salad that does not meet certain standards. Whether a salad is classified as an appetizer, an entree, accompaniment, or dessert, or whether it is served individually, on a large buffet tray or in the salad bowl, the same general rules hold for all.

All uncooked materials must be crisp, cold, and free from excess moisture. They should be artfully blended and served on chilled plates.

Salad greens must be fresh, crisp, and pleasing to the eye. Accent light greens with dark parsley, watercress, mint leaves, or other suitable edible greens. For variety, dip edges of leaves in paprika.

Use materials that produce a contrast in texture, flavor, and color.

Arrange the salad attractively with some definite pattern in mind.

Garnishes should be gay and appetizing, though simple and not overworked. They are usually a part of the salad.

In general, use small garnishes for individual salads and large garnishes for the buffet salad tray or salad bowl.

Do not overgarnish!

Fruits

APPLES Balls Scoop balls from firm apples with a French fruit or vegetable cutter. Place balls in a water or sugar solution colored with pure fruit coloring. When the desired tint is obtained, remove balls from liquid, drain, and dry well. Arrange in groups on salad greens, with or without the use of toothpicks.

Variation Dip apple balls in pineapple juice, then drain. Insert a toothpick in each ball. When balls are dry, paint each one with a paintbrush, using pure fruit coloring. Vary the color combinations and designs.

Cups Use red- or yellow-skinned unpeeled apples. When using small apples, cut slice from blossom end, scoop out pulp, and scallop edges with a sharp knife. Dip in pineapple juice, drain, dry edges, then dip edges in powdered sugar, if desired. Fill with any of the following:

Fresh Fruits in Season: Blueberries, cranberries (whole cooked fruit or molded jelly cut in shapes), currants, ground cherries, strawberries.

Canned Fruit: Whole small fruit, or large fruit, diced.
Dressing: Serve with spoon carved from carrot or cucumber.

Arrange the apple cups on a bed of greens around a salad, use singly at center of interest, or in groups, depending upon size of salad tray and type of salad.

When using large apples, follow direction for *apple cups* in meat section. Fill with any fruit or salad combination desired.

Rings Cut red- or yellow-skinned cooking apples into ⅓ to ½ inch slices. Tint red, green, or yellow by allowing slices to stand in sirup solution colored with fruit coloring.

For mint flavor, add a drop of oil of peppermint to sirup.

For cinnamon flavor, add a piece of stick cinnamon to sirup.

TOP APPLE RINGS WITH:

Red or green candied cherries used whole, halved, or in sections to form petals.
Dates cut in strips or stuffed and sliced.

Maraschino cherries used in the same way as candied cherries.
Raisins.

Strips Cut apples into matchlike strips, then place in water or sirup solution colored with fruit coloring. When tinted, remove from liquid, drain, and dry. Arrange assorted colors in interesting groups on salad greens. Serve immediately.

APRICOTS Cut fresh or canned apricots in sections to form petals. Arrange in design on salad with or without mint leaves. Use a slice of date or large raisin for center of flower.

Fill canned or fresh apricot halves with small fruit in season, such as blackberries, blueberries, currants, dewberries, gooseberries, grapes, loganberries, strawberries, or thimbleberries.

Arrange as a border or place in groups on large salad tray.

Use apricot halves with the cut surface down. Cut blanched almonds into matchlike strips, then insert in outer surface of apricot halves. These are effective in deep greens.

Fill apricot halves with shredded coconut or walnut halves.

AVOCADOS Cut one slice from the blossom end of the

fruit. Remove seed; fill with a tart fruit
gelatin mixture of contrasting color. Replace slice and chill until firm. Slice about
1 inch thick, then cut each slice into six
or eight segments, depending upon size of
fruit. Arrange around salad with the point
of each segment facing the outer rim of
the plate.

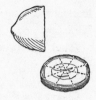

BANANAS Score a peeled banana by drawing the prongs
of a fork lengthwise down the outer surface. Slice crosswise or
at an angle. Dip in pineapple juice, drain, then dip outer edge
of banana in chopped mint leaves or chopped parsley. Place
in flat or upright position, petal fashion, on slice of orange.

BERRIES Arrange clusters of blackberries, blueberries, raspberries, thimbleberries, boysenberries, loganberries, or dewberries at center of interest on individual or general salad.

Use strawberries, with or without hulls, singly or in clusters.

Scatter sliced strawberries over fruit salad.

Arrange clusters of gooseberries or currants on top of
melon-ball salad.

CHERRIES Use candied, maraschino, or mint cherries.
Candied and maraschino cherries may be obtained in either
red or green colors, with or without stems.

Top salads with a whole, half, or a slice of cherry. Use
singly or in groups to form design.

Cut cherry into petals, and arrange in flower design on top
or at side of salad. Use sprig of mint or citron to form stem
and leaves. A cluster of three cherry flowers without stems and
leaves makes an attractive garnish.

Cut cherries in eighths and use segments to form dividing

line between grapefruit sections placed close to each other in salad.

Insert small end of a whole blanched, toasted, and salted almond in cherry cavity. Use one or more as needed for proper balance on salad.

Cherry flower. See directions for cherries in appetizer section.

Bing cherries are effective used singly or in groups, or in cavity of larger fruits, such as pears, peaches, or in center of pineapple ring.

CRANBERRIES Place cranberry bouquets at base of salad on large tray. See directions for making bouquet appetizers in appetizer section, using cranberries on toothpicks.

Top salads with bells, stars, or other shapes cut from cranberry jelly.

DATES Stuff dates with cream cheese, peanut butter, or nut meats. Use whole or sliced. Slices of cheese-filled dates may be overlapped to form a circle or other geometric design.

Cut dates in lengthwise strips and arrange petal fashion on slice of pineapple or combination fruit salad. Use a small round of candied orange peel for the center of the flower.

FIGS Cut pressed figs into tiny pieces with a scissors, then sprinkle lightly over center of salad; or make a solid border near base of salad.

Arrange strips of pressed figs around a colored gumdrop on a light-colored salad.

GRAPEFRUIT Cups Trace a ½-inch band circling the middle portions of a whole grapefruit. Then trace rounded scallops within this band. Cut scallops through to center of fruit. When all lines have been cut, separate fruit into two scalloped cups. Scoop out the pulp. Punch each scallop with a paper punch to give a lacy effect, or use a fruit cutter (a special gadget which punches and cuts grapefruit or other peel into lacy scallops in one operation). Fill the cups with melon balls or cubed fresh or canned fruit, or small whole fruits in season. Place on galax leaves or other greens. Insert a sprig or two of mint near rim of cup.

Baskets   For directions for orange baskets, see Index. Fill with fruit or vegetable combination salad.

Bow   Cut a slice of grapefruit ¼ to ⅓ inch wide crosswise through middle section of fruit. Remove the pulp carefully so that the peel will stay intact. Bring the two sides of the peel together to form a bow and fasten with a tiny piece of toothpick and greens, or a strip of pimiento. Place bow over salad in grapefruit bowl or arrange on large general salad. A maraschino cherry may be placed on each side of the center of the bow to lend color and interest to the garnish.

Sections   Arrange with clusters of Bing cherries on tossed green or molded salad.

Cubes   Combine grapefruit cubes or wedges with fruit gelatin cubes of contrasting color. Place in nests of shredded lettuce as a border around salad.

GRAPES   Frosted   For directions, see Helpful Hints in section on general directions. Place frosted grapes on bed of greens next to a molded colorful gelatin salad.

Colored Grapes   Small green, red, or orange grapes are available in bottles. Arrange in design or in clusters with or without mint leaves.

Remove stems from fresh assorted grapes; place in nests of

shredded lettuce, endive, or watercress. Small nests about 1½ inches in diameter are suitable for individual salads.

Cut grapes in half lengthwise, remove seeds, arrange petal fashion on top or at sides of combination fruit salad or molded salad.

Place canned pear half on a bed of watercress. Frost surface of pear with cream cheese or smooth cottage cheese. Completely cover the cheese frosting with grapes cut in half lengthwise and seeded, so that the pear will resemble a bunch of grapes.

KUMQUATS   Use fresh whole kumquats either singly or in groups of 3 near base of salad among the greens.

Cut a slice from one end of a kumquat, remove some of the pulp, and stuff with tinted coconut. Arrange as a border around salad.

Cut a slice from one end of kumquat, remove pulp, and fill with green or red fruit gelatin. Chill until firm; cut into slices about ¼ inch thick, then cut each slice into wedges, starting from the center and cutting down to but not through the rind except in one place. Take one end of rind and gently form a circle with rind on the inside and the points of the wedges extending outward like a diadem.

Overlap slices of kumquats in groups of three or five on molded salads or in salad greens.

LEMONS OR LIMES Baskets   See directions for lemons in meat section. Fill with any small fruit in season, and use with a salad of contrasting color. Lemon or lime cups or baskets filled with melon balls and mint leaves make attractive garnishes.

Slices   Use lemon or lime slices in any of the following ways:

Cut lemon slice into geometric design.

Remove pulp from a section of a lemon slice and curl freed rind.

Cut a slice about ⅛ inch thick, then cut through rind and up to center of slice. Twist free ends in opposite directions.

Coat entire slice of lemon with chopped parsley or chives and arrange on salad.

Stuffed   Cut a small slice from blossom end of a well-shaped lemon or lime. Scoop out the pulp; dry well. Fill with gelatin mixture that is stiffer than usual. Pour into lemon cups when gelatin is about ready to congeal. Chill until firm. Cut in slices, quarters, or wedges. Lime, cherry, or strawberry gelatin makes an attractive filling.

MELONS   Scoop balls from watermelon, muskmelon, or honeydew melon with a French ball cutter. Alternate in groups of 3 or 5 in greens as a border around a large general salad. For variety, mix different melon balls in each group.

Tint honeydew melon balls orange, red, or green to suit color scheme, or paint them with a paintbrush and pure fruit coloring. Place in nests of shredded lettuce to resemble Easter eggs. The melon balls may also be attached to toothpicks and inserted in sides of salad in some definite design.

Cube melon; combine with fresh blueberries and serve in lemon cups.

Use peeled or unpeeled honeydew or muskmelon. Cut a slice from one end; scoop out seeds and membrane. Fill with fruit or vegetable gelatin of contrasting color. Make gelatin a little stiffer than usual. Replace top slice and chill melon until gelatin is firm. If peeled melon has been used, score with a fluting knife before cutting slices or frost with softened cream cheese or cream cottage cheese. When firm, cut in slices. If slices are small, use whole; if large, cut in wedges and arrange as border around a general salad.

OLIVES   Garnish salads with whole olives, used singly or in groups.

Cut stuffed olives into slices and arrange in design.

Cut a whole olive into sections, being careful not to cut through the base of the olive. Gently remove the stone and place cup-shaped flower on salad. Place a piece of cheese in the center, or fill with pimiento, tinted cream cheese, or mayonnaise forced through a pastry tube. This garnish resembles a water lily. A group arranged on a light-colored salad is very effective.

Remove pimiento from stuffed olive; insert blanched salted almond.

ORANGES   **Baskets and Cups**   Follow directions for lemons in meat section. Fill with melon balls or small fruit in season and arrange on large salad trays. These fruit cups are suitable containers for many individual combination salads.

Slices   Top orange slices with whole nut meats or with white grapes and a sprig of mint.

Candied Peel   Orange, lemon, or grapefruit peel may be candied in the following way. Cut the peel into quarters, then into slices about 1 inch wide. Cover with cold water and bring to a boil; cook about 3 minutes. Drain; add cold water to cover, and cook another 3 minutes. Repeat a third time. Measure peel; add an equal amount of sugar. Cook until very thick. While hot, sprinkle with sugar. If available, use green, red, orange, or blue sugar. For colored peel, add a few drops of fruit or vegetable coloring while peel is cooking. The peel may be chopped or cut into strips or flowers.

Pickled Peel   Cook rind as for candied peel, then drain. Boil together 4 cups sugar, 2 cups vinegar, and 2 tablespoons pickling spices for 5 minutes. Add peel; cook, stirring occasionally, for about 1¼ hours. This amount will make 3 pints of pickled peel that can be used as needed. Stud with whole cloves and place on salad.

Stuffed Oranges   Boil whole seedless oranges until quite tender; cool, then cut in half. Scoop out some of the pulp and fill with a mixture of chopped nuts, crystallized ginger, and candied cherries. If necessary, add sugar to sweeten. Place orange halves in a shallow pan and pour 1 cup of sirup over them. (To make the sirup, boil 1 cup sugar with ¾ cup water for 10 minutes.) Glaze in a hot oven. Top with maraschino cherry and serve as a garnish on large salad trays.

Trace a 5-petaled flower on the peel of an orange with the stem end as the base of the flower. Peel the orange, cutting the petals three fourths of the way down. Remove the pulp; cube and mix with other fruit in season. Fill the petal-shaped orange basket with the fruit salad and arrange on a bed of greens. Top with two or three mint leaves.

PEACHES   Fill canned peach halves with spiced whole cranberries, cranberry jelly, cottage cheese, cheese balls rolled in chopped parsley or nut meats, Bing cherries, blueberries, or other small fruit in season.

Place peach halves upside down in greens on salad tray. Stud with whole cloves in a definite design. Letters and numbers may be formed in this manner.

Remove stone from whole spiced peach and fill cavity with creamed cottage cheese, either plain or mixed with small pieces of dates or chopped chives. Place on top of a slice of pineapple, round side up, or on a flat gelatin mold. Use gumdrops to form eyes, nose, and mouth, or cloves for the eyes and a section of maraschino cherry for the mouth. If candy is used, attach each piece to a small piece of toothpick and insert into the peach. To

make a clown for Halloween, use a long gumdrop for the mouth with a molded cream cheese tooth here and there. Pipe a collar around the neck with yellow-tinted cream cheese. Put black dots on the collar, using bits of black gumdrop, a pressed fig on the peach head for the brim of the hat, and a half marshmallow for the crown. If desired, the crown may be decorated with slivers of gumdrops.

PEARS Tint a number of canned pear halves pink and an equal number green by allowing them to stand in their own juice in separate dishes, one tinted pink, the other green. Use pure fruit coloring. When the desired color is obtained, drain, then fill cavity with well-seasoned cream cheese and press one pink half to a green half. Use a sprig of mint at stem end and a whole clove at blossom end. Place in bed of greens.

Tint two pear halves yellow, two pink, and two green. Fill the cavities with cottage cheese. Fasten the halves of the same color together. Insert a piece of green pepper for stem and clove for blossom end. Arrange in border around a salad.

Turkey Place a large canned pear half, cut side down, on lettuce. (If medium or small pear halves are used, fasten the two halves together with cream cheese for the body of the turkey). Use plain or roll in graham cracker crumbs or ground  nut meats. Fit two thirds of a pineapple slice over small end of pear for the tail and insert a segment of red-skinned apple, ½ to ¾ inch wide and 3 or more inches long, through large end of pear for the neck. Place a cherry on top of the apple wedge for the head and a piece of date for the beak. Let a tiny piece of red cherry dangle over beak for the wattle of the turkey. Very effective when served as an individual salad.

Fill tinted canned pear halves with cheese balls that have been tinted a contrasting color. The balls may be formed with two or more kinds of colored cheese.

Fill pear cavity with Bing cherries, blueberries, raspberries, or other small fruit in season.

Fill pear cavity with fruit gelatin cubes or shirred gelatin, blending two or more colors together. To shir gelatin, mold a thin layer in a shallow pan. When firm, cut with the prongs of a fork.

Easter Bunny   Use large canned pear half. Place cut side down on shredded lettuce. Insert two cloves or tiny pink candies for eyes at small end of pear. Use fruit coloring to paint a pink streak down  middle of blanched almonds for inner part of ear. Insert two of these streaked almonds in back of the eyes for ears. Place a piece of raisin or maraschino cherry in the pear for the mouth. Cut the dry powdered surface from a tender marshmallow and use the cottony ball remaining for the tail.

PERSIMMON   Cut persimmon into cubes and marinate in French dressing. Drain well and place on top of a light-colored salad.

Slice a persimmon and place a small pitted prune, plain or stuffed, in the center of each slice. Arrange in groups on large salad tray.

Cut a persimmon petal fashion and arrange on large buffet salad. Use a crosswise slice of date or prune as the center of the flower.

PINEAPPLE   Place a slice of cranberry jelly on a slice of pineapple; top with cream cheese forced through a pastry tube.

Color pineapple green, red, or orange by allowing pineapple rings to stand in pineapple juice to which fruit coloring has been added. Use slices whole or cut in wedges.

Candles   Cut a banana in half crosswise and use a half for each candle. Stand the banana in the center of a pineapple ring. Top with mayonnaise and maraschino cherry. Arrange on large salad tray. Birthday candles placed in candy candle-holders may be inserted in pineapple ring and lighted just before serving. Arrange in groups of three at each end of a long salad tray.

Place ripe olives or Bing cherries in center of pineapple ring with a sprig of mint.

Top slice of pineapple with cone-shaped scoop of cottage cheese. Alternate green pepper and pimiento strips around cheese in spiral fashion.

Insert whole cloves in outer edge of pineapple ring near rim on top of the slice, or use cloves to form design on top of the slice.

Pineapple Fingers Use canned or candied pineapple. To make candied pineapple, boil 2 cups sugar, ⅓ cup sirup, and 1 cup water together until the sirup spins a thread when dropped from a spoon (234–236° F.). Add dry pineapple slices or fingers to the sirup and cook until fruit is clear. Remove from sirup, drain, spread on wire rack to dry until fruit is no longer sticky. Pack between sheets of waxed paper and place in a tin box or glass jar until ready to use.

POMEGRANATE SEEDS Sprinkle pomegranate seeds over salad or mix with tossed green salad. These seeds may be used to simulate holly berries, combined with citron leaves, and arranged around pear cavity or on pineapple ring.

PLUMS Arrange fresh whole plums singly or in groups on large salad trays.

Cut large, firm plum in half lengthwise, remove pit, and stuff the cavity with well-seasoned cottage cheese.

Section prune plums lengthwise and arrange on salad in

petal fashion. Use a tiny round piece of fresh orange rind for center of flower.

PRUNES   Stuff pitted prunes with creamed cottage cheese, marshmallow, chopped dates, nut meats, pineapple, or orange sections.

Stand three blanched toasted almonds upright in pitted prunes. Place on a slice of fruit or in bed of greens.

RAISINS   Use dark or light raisins, dried or steamed, singly in design, or in groups on fruit slices or salad greens.

RHUBARB   Peel rhubarb as thinly as possible. Peel will curl up naturally. Arrange curls on bed of salad greens.

Vegetables

BEANS   Cook whole green or wax beans cut in julienne strips. Marinate in sweet-sour dressing and drain. Use as a garnish on vegetable salads, or combine with cooked julienne carrots.

BEETS   Slice sweet pickled beets, then cut into crescents, stars, animals, or other shapes. Place on or around salad just before serving.

Cut a slice from root end of cooked beet, scoop out pulp, and fill with any desired salad or salad dressing.

Stuff beet cups with cream cheese or gelatin of contrasting

color. When firm, cut in slices or sections and use around meat, fish, or vegetable salads.

Cut lattice slices with a fluting knife. For directions, see lattice potatoes in directions for potatoes in fish section.

Cut beet slices crosswise with a fluting knife, to form julienne strips.

Shred raw or cooked beets. Be sure to follow grain of beet when shredding. Arrange in mounds or combine with raw shredded turnips to form border.

BROCCOLI   Cook fresh broccoli until tender but firm. Separate floret for individual salad, or use large bunch for large salad tray. Marinate broccoli before using.

BRUSSELS SPROUTS   Cook, drain, marinate in sweet-sour dressing, then drain again. Serve whole or sliced on salad.

CABBAGE   Chop raw red and green cabbage and marinate in sweet-sour dressing, or juice from sweet-sour pickles. Drain, then form into nests, using each color separately. Alternate red and green nests around salad tray. Fill nests with marinated vegetables, meat balls, or cheese balls.

CARROTS   Shred carrots with the grain of the vegetable. Top salads with small bunches of shredded carrots or form border around salad.

Cut a carrot in half lengthwise, then cut very thin lengthwise slices from middle portion. Fringe edges of both sides of slice about ¼ inch deep. Cuts may be made either straight or diagonally. Curl slices, fasten with a toothpick, and place in ice water to chill.

Make nests with shredded carrots, fill with plain or tinted melon balls, cream-cheese balls, or balls cut from other suitable vegetables.

Sprinkle grated carrot over salad.

Flowers For brown-eyed Susans, cut a ⅛ inch slice from large end of carrot. Place a daisy cardboard pattern on top, trace, and cut. Place small round piece of date or truffle in center of flower. For variation of this flower and for carrot jonquils, see directions for flowers in meat section.

For other flowers, cut carrot slices with various flower cutters. Fasten each flower to end of toothpick and arrange in salad greens.

Press a shrimp cutter through center of large carrot. Cut in 2-inch sections, cook, or use raw as a salad garnish. For variety, unwind shrimp strands and rewind with potato shrimp cut in the same way.

CELERY Pull a 4-inch stalk of celery through a carrot ring. Fringe each end of celery stalk down about 1½ inches on each side.

Stuff celery with tinted cream cheese, using layers of different-colored cheese. Cut in slices to obtain a rainbow effect and scatter over salad.

CHIVES Chop fine and sprinkle over salad.

Cut chive stalks in rings; scatter over light-colored vegetable salad.

CUCUMBERS Score a peeled cucumber with a fluting knife or by drawing a fork lengthwise over outer surface. Slice, and marinate in French or sweet-sour dressing. Drain, then arrange on salad and sprinkle with paprika.

Form cucumber chain by cutting slices from peeled or unpeeled cucumber about ⅛ inch wide. Remove pulp to form rings. Make one cut through the rind in all but the first ring. Fit one ring into the other through the cut in rind. Arrange around salad.

Baskets See directions for cucumbers in fish section.

Boats Use a 4- to 5-inch cucumber. Cut off a lengthwise slice; scoop out center portion. Fill with combination salad. Carve oars out of carrot slices and fasten to side of cucumber boat. Cut sail from turnip slice.

Cucumber Twists See directions for cucumbers in fish section.

Cucumber Curls See directions for cucumbers in fish section.

Cucumber Water Lily See directions for cucumbers in fish section.

Cucumber Rose See directions for cucumbers in fish section.

Arrange three slices of scored unpeeled cucumber on salad plate and top with a round mold of tomato jelly. Place a few mint leaves at base of mold and two or three leaves on top.

Score any firm vegetables, slice, and combine in groups of three or more slices of graduated sizes. Use scored, unpeeled cucumber slices in these groups.

ONIONS Interlace white or tinted onion rings on tossed salad.

Fill nests of greens or shredded carrots with pearl onions. Or arrange onions in border around salad.

Scatter bird's-eye onions over salad.

Marinate cooked onion cups and fill with cubed pickled beets. Arrange in groups of three on large salad tray.

PARSLEY   Chop parsley and sprinkle over salad.

Arrange sprigs or tiny sections of parsley in appropriate setting on salad.

PEPPERS   Fill red or green pepper cases with gelatin salad. When firm, slice or cut in wedges and arrange around large salad.

Fill pepper cases with cottage cheese and cut in slices or wedges. Use as garnish for salad tray.

Cut pepper cases in half, remove seeds and membrane, scallop edges, and fill with marinated vegetable balls.

POTATO FLOWER BASKET   Peel large potatoes and slice paper thin. Cut into strips 1 inch wide and 2½ inches long; cut one end to a point. Place seven petals in outer part of small frying basket; hold in place while inserting inside basket. Fry in deep fat to a golden brown. Remove carefully from basket. Serve colored cheese balls or melon balls in the potato basket. Arrange on large salad tray.

POTATO CHIPS   Dip half of each potato chip in cream cheese-mayonnaise dressing which has been flavored with horse-radish and onion to suit taste. Arrange around salad. To make dressing, cream 1 3-ounce package of cream cheese until light and fluffy, mix well with ½ cup mayonnaise, then add 1 tablespoon (more or less, as desired) of horse-radish and ½ teaspoon grated onion. Add salt if necessary.

Dip edges of potato chips in paprika, then form flower design in center of each chip with tinted cream cheese forced through pastry tube. Place in groups at end of salad tray.

Dip edges of potato chips in mayonnaise, then in paprika or chopped chives. For variation, dip edges of chips in softened colored cream cheese.

RADISHES   Radish Rose, Tulip, or Fan   See directions for radishes in appetizer section.

Water Lily   Outline five petals on the surface of a radish to resemble a water lily. Use the stem end as the base. Cut petals down to within ¼ inch of the base. Scoop out pulp. Insert a round of red radish peel or orange peel for center of flower. The large end of white icicle radishes may be cut in the same way. Chill in ice water; drain; dry; dip edges in paprika.

RUTABAGA   Jonquils   See directions for flowers in meat section.

SCALLIONS   Trim scallions, then slice or chop and scatter over salad. Scallions are both attractive and tasty on tossed green salads.

TOMATOES   Cut a small or medium-sized whole tomato in five sections, starting from blossom end and cutting far enough to spread sections slightly (a little more than halfway). Sprinkle sieved cooked yolk in center of flower thus formed.

Cut tomato in wedges and arrange petal fashion around half of a hard-cooked egg. Stand egg half on end so yolk is in view.

Tomato Rose Cup   Trace petals or deep scallops on a firm ripe tomato. Cut tracings with a sharp knife. Scoop out center sufficiently to hold thick salad dressing.

Tomato Cheese Rose   Use medium-sized tomato. See directions for tomatoes in appetizer section.

Tomato Candle   Peel a medium-sized, firm tomato and place in lettuce cup, blossom end up. With an apple corer remove enough pulp to admit one marinated asparagus tip. Cut a handle for the candleholder from an unpeeled cucumber slice. Insert in the side of the tomato. If cucumbers are not available, make the handle out of green pepper.

TRUFFLES   Chop or cut in fancy shapes. Used mostly for accent and to bring out the other colors in flowers or designs.

TURNIPS   Daisies and Narcissus   See directions for flowers in meat section.

Tulips   Use a turnip about 3 inches long and about 2 inches wide at the base. Trace five tulip petals on the surface of the turnip, using the stem end as the base of the flower. Cut the petals with a thin, sharp knife, then place in ice water until ready to serve.

Cut animals or other objects from turnip slices. Use fancy cutters or place a cardboard pattern on the turnip slice and cut out design with a sharp knife. Place turnip cutouts on top of molded salad of darker background, or mold them into the salad in some attractive design.

With a shrimp knife cut two long curled sections from a cooked turnip. Unwind, and interchange colors with cooked beets cut in the same manner.

VEGETABLE CORSAGE   Make narcissus, daisies, jonquils, and brown-eyed Susans out of turnips, rutabagas, and carrots. (See directions for flowers in meat section.) Combine with parsley or mint leaves and arrange on large salad tray.

Other Salad Garnishes

ANCHOVIES   Arrange anchovy fillets in design on fish salad.

ANGELICA   Cut in shape of leaves or tiny dots. Use to accent light decoration, such as whipped-cream mayonnaise.

ASPIC   Color well-seasoned aspic with vegetable coloring. Chill until firm and cut into cubes or fancy shapes. Place in center of salad or arrange on greens as border.

CAPERS   Use sparingly, either whole or chopped.

CHEESE   **Special Molds**   Use softened processed cheese or grated American cheese to form any of the following:

Christmas   Make tiny cribs, animals, Santas, trees, stockings, or toys. Paint with vegetable coloring. Place objects on top or side of molded salad.

Easter   Form eggs, baby chicks, rabbits, lambs, or lilies. Paint with vegetable coloring and use same as above.

Thanksgiving   Make turkeys, pumpkins, or various fruits and vegetables. Paint with vegetable coloring. A variety of fruits and vegetables may be arranged as a border on salad tray.

St. Patrick's Day   Form shamrocks and pipes. Paint shamrocks with vegetable coloring.

George Washington's Birthday   Mold cherries, logs, or hatchets. Arrange in units on salad tray.

Any or all of these motifs may also be cut from slices of American cheese and painted to resemble the various objects.

Bonbons Mold processed cheese into balls, then press blanched almonds, pecan or walnut halves, or pistachio nut meats into top of cheese balls.

Strawberries Form cheese into the shape of strawberries, dust with paprika, and place tiny mint or other suitable leaf at stem end for hull.

EGGS See directions for eggs in appetizer, fish, and meat sections.

Hard-cooked eggs may be sliced, quartered, or stuffed and sprinkled with paprika or minced parsley, chives, or olives. They also may be riced, using white and yolk separately or combined, or the egg whites may be cut in julienne strips.

Sieve egg yolk on beet slices, or top egg-white slices with sieved egg yolk.

Prepare deviled eggs; cut in sections, slices, or halves, or fit halves together. Place pimiento and green-pepper strips alternately over deviled eggs.

Cut egg white into petals to form daisy or other flower design. Use sieved yolk for center of flowers.

Egg Cups Cut hard-cooked eggs in half crosswise or lengthwise with a thin, sharp knife. The edges may be scalloped by cutting the egg in half with a fluting knife. Start at one point, cut up to the center, turn the egg, and cut again. Make each cut to the center but not through it, and repeat until the egg separates into two equal parts. If colored cups are desired, paint each one in the same or contrasting colors with pure fruit coloring.

FLOWERS Arrange a spray of bright-colored flowers in a bed of greens next to a somewhat colorless salad. Fragrant fresh flowers or candied flowers may be used.

GELATIN   Pour gelatin into a flat pan to a depth of ⅓ to ½ inch. Allow to congeal, then cut in any shape desired, such as cubes, animals, stars, hearts, shamrocks, hatchets, or any other design that will carry out a seasonal idea.

Combine two or more colors of shirred gelatin and place on top of combination fruit salads or on top of whipped-cream mayonnaise.

HORSE-RADISH   Fill small colorful cooked vegetable cups with ground, well-seasoned horse-radish.

LOBSTER   Garnish lobster salad with lobster claws, feelers, or corals. Use on large salad trays.

NUT MEATS   Form design with whole or half nut meats.

Combine nut meats with fruits, and arrange in design on salad.

PAPRIKA   Use sparingly; sprinkle over salads.

PICKLES   See directions for pickles in appetizer section.

Top salads with cucumber pickles, either whole, halves, quarters, or slices. Arrange in design.

Cut sweet-sour pickle slices in fancy shapes.

Cut cucumber pickles diagonally with fluting knife, arrange the slices in upright position, petal fashion, on top of salad.

PRESERVED GINGER   Chop, cut into strips or rounds, and arrange in design on salad.

SALAD DRESSING Tint your favorite mayonnaise or whipped-cream dressing and pipe on salads.

Make a salad dressing with melted vegetable shortening instead of oil, add desired coloring, then continue as for mayonnaise. Chill; cut in various shapes, such as cubes, balls, chickens, or whatever is suitable for the occasion.

Place a mint leaf or sprig on top of Russian or rather thick French dressing.

Arrange sections of a cherry in a flower design on top of mayonnaise or thick salad dressing.

SARDINES Decorate fish salads with whole sardines topped with pimiento strips.

SHRIMP Remove black vein from shrimp. Pipe colored cream cheese in space left after removal of vein. Arrange on oak-leaf lettuce or on fish salad in definite design.

WHIPPED CREAM Force white or tinted whipped cream through pastry tube to form rosettes or other designs on salads.

Combine whipped cream with mayonnaise or cooked salad dressing made with fruit juice. Chill the dressing before combining with whipped cream.

Scatter bits of candied fruit on whipped-cream-mayonnaise dressing.

Sandwiches

ANCHOVIES Pipe anchovy paste on or around open-faced sandwiches. The paste may be made in one of two ways. Cream and blend 2 tablespoons butter with ½ teaspoon anchovy paste as purchased. Or rub yolks of 2 cooked eggs to a smooth paste, combine with 2 boned and mashed anchovies, ¼ cup butter, and a few grains of paprika.

BACON Break grilled bacon into bits; sprinkle over individual open-faced sandwiches. The small bacon pieces may also be used to form a design on a frosted sandwich loaf.

BAKED BEAN PASTE Pipe baked bean paste in rows on white bread; alternate rows with a light-colored spread, or completely cover finger strips of Boston brown bread. To make the paste, mash 1 cup baked beans to a paste and season with 3 tablespoons tomato catsup, chili sauce, or 1 teaspoon mustard. One tablespoon of onion juice may be added if desired.

CARROTS   Cut raw carrot in various shapes and arrange on open-face sandwiches which are spread with a well-seasoned mixture.

CAVIAR   Form in rows, circles, or other designs. Use a combination of one or more colors.

CELERY   Cut stuffed celery in thin slices; arrange in design on open-faced sandwiches; spread with anchovy paste or savory butter.

CHEESE   Pipe cream-cheese or cottage-cheese spreads in the form of borders or geometric designs on open-faced sandwiches.

Suggested Preparations   Combine 1 cup cheese with 1 minced pimiento; 1 tablespoon minced chives; 2 tablespoons minced pimiento olives and 1 tablespoon mayonnaise; or 2 to 4 tablespoons minced red and green pepper and 1 tablespoon mayonnaise.

Combine ½ cup cheese with 3 tablespoons chopped dates or date paste and minced raisins; or add 1 tablespoon mayonnaise and ¼ cup chopped pecans.

Spread open-faced sandwiches with cream or cottage cheese, then top with a layer of strawberry or raspberry jam, orange marmalade, or finely chopped salted peanuts.

Combine ¼ cup cheese, ¼ cup chopped cucumber, and ½ cup chopped raisins.

Tint cream or cottage cheese with vegetable coloring before decorating sandwiches.

Cut American cheese in various shapes. Arrange on sandwich loaves or open-faced sandwiches.

CHOCOLATE PASTE   Use as spread or piping on graham crackers or other sweet crackers or bread. To make chocolate paste, combine 4 tablespoons butter, ¾ cup confectioners' sugar, 2 squares (1 ounce) bitter chocolate, melted, ¼ teaspoon cinnamon, ½ teaspoon vanilla. Mix until smooth and well blended.

CRANBERRIES   Use whole cooked cranberries in center or around the edge as border on sandwich.

Cut cranberry jelly in various shapes and arrange on open-faced sandwiches or frosted sandwich loaves.

CURRANTS   Use fresh or dried currants to form a border or a geometric design on cheese-covered sandwiches.

DATES   Cut in the shape of petals and arrange in a flower design on open-faced sandwiches or on frosted sandwich loaves.

Cut dates into small pieces and use to form a border or other design.

Use date paste as a spread or pipe around edge of sandwich. To make date paste, mince 1 cup dates and add 1 tablespoon orange juice and ⅛ teaspoon cinnamon. Blend well.

EGGS   Use hard-cooked eggs and sieve yolk and white separately. Sprinkle over the design of a cardboard stencil which has been placed over bread covered with savory spread. Remove cardboard gently to obtain a perfect pattern.

Form rosettes or other designs on bread with egg-yolk paste forced through a pastry tube. To make paste, blend ¼ cup butter, 2 hard-cooked egg yolks, a few grains of paprika, and a few drops of tabasco sauce.

Rainbow Sandwich   Mince 2 hard-cooked eggs and combine with 1 tablespoon chopped pickle relish and enough mayonnaise to hold ingredients together. Add salt to taste. Chopped olives and pecan nut meats may be added if desired. Cut round  Bohemian rye bread into slices 12 inches in diameter. To obtain slices of this size cut the bread horizontally, starting from the top. Spread a 1-inch circle near the center of the slice with the egg mixture and alternate with 1-inch circles of minced-ham spread. Place rosettes of yellow-tinted cream cheese in the center of the slice of bread and form border with either chopped parsley or green-tinted cream cheese. Flute the edges of the completed sandwich.

FIGS   Chop or cut figs into strips or rounds and arrange in a design on open-faced sandwich.

GINGER   Sprinkle chopped ginger over sandwich covered with tasty spread or form border or other design.

GRAPES   Cut grapes in half, seed, and arrange in pattern on sandwich loaf or open-faced sandwich.

GREENS   Chop chives, parsley, or young onion tops and arrange in a border or design, or sprinkle over sandwich covered with a tasty spread.

Top sandwich with a section of red cherry and two mint leaves arranged on opposite sides of cherry.

Arrange sprigs of watercress around sandwich loaf. Use small sprigs for top of loaf and larger sprigs at base.

Place a small head of oak-leaf lettuce in center of sandwich tray; place sandwiches on lettuce of the same variety.

Use chicory (curly endive) as a colorful border or center for a sandwich tray.

MARASCHINO OR CANDIED CHERRIES Arrange chopped cherries in design on an open-faced sandwich.

Cut red and green cherries in petal-shaped sections, then alternate the sections on an open-faced sandwich.

MARSHMALLOWS Use whole, halves, or sections of marshmallows on either white or dark bread. For additional color use tinted marshmallows. Heat just enough to puff before serving.

NASTURTIUMS Top sandwiches with fresh nasturtium blossoms and leaves.

NUT MEATS Sprinkle chopped nut meats over sandwich or arrange in design.

Top sandwiches with whole nut meats or nut-meat halves.

OLIVES Slice stuffed olives, or cut in halves, and arrange in design.

Chop ripe or green olives and use to form border on sandwich.

ONIONS Overlap tinted onion rings on sandwich covered with a tasty spread.

PAPRIKA   Roll edges of bread in paprika, or sprinkle paprika over cheese-spread sandwich.

PARSLEY   Decorate sandwiches with parsley paste forced through decorating tube. To make paste, cream 2 tablespoons butter and add 1 tablespoon finely chopped parsley. Mix thoroughly.

PEANUT SPREAD   Wash and grind ¼ cup figs and ¼ cup raisins. Add ½ teaspoon salt, ½ cup peanut butter, 2 tablespoons corn sirup, and 2 tablespoons lemon juice. Mix well. Spread in rows on oblong sandwich or in two circles on round shapes.

Mix ½ cup peanut butter and ¼ cup cream until smooth and light in color. Spread on slice of bread and top with layer of orange marmalade. The marmalade may also be mixed with the peanut butter and cream. Use ¼ cup marmalade with the above proportions.

PEPPERS   Chop red or green pepper or cut into strips. Arrange the latter in parallel lines on egg-salad sandwich.

PICKLES   Score sweet-sour pickles, then slice. Place on closed or open-faced sandwiches or on frosted sandwich loaf.

Cut pickles into strips and form designs on sandwiches.

Chop pickles. Place a cardboard stencil over sandwiches covered with a savory spread. Sprinkle chopped pickles over the stencil design, then remove cardboard carefully.

PIMIENTO   Chop or cut pimiento into strips and arrange in a design.

Cut crescents, stars, flowers, or other objects from pimiento and arrange on frosted sandwich loaf or open-faced sandwiches.

PINEAPPLE Tint strips or crushed pineapple green, red, or orange. Drain well, and use in designs on open-faced sandwiches. To tint pineapple, allow the fruit to stand in its own juice which has been colored with pure fruit coloring.

RAISINS Use raisins whole or cut into tiny pieces. They are usually combined with fruits of other colors when used in designs.

TRUFFLES Chop truffles or cut into fancy shapes. Place on sandwich loaf or on open-faced sandwiches.

TURNIPS Cut in shapes of animals, flowers, or other objects and place on sandwiches covered with colorful spreads.

MISCELLANEOUS SUGGESTIONS Use checkerboard, ribbon, and rolled sandwiches which have been filled with colorful spreads to add beauty to the sandwich tray.

Checkerboard Sandwiches Use filling that will adhere to the bread. Cut four slices of bread about ½ inch thick. Spread with filling and form two stacks, one beginning with white bread, the other beginning with dark bread. Cut crosswise through each stack. (This will form ribbon 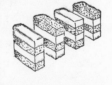 sandwiches.) Take a slice of ribbon sandwich which has dark bread at the top, cover it with sandwich spread, and place on top of it a second ribbon sandwich with white bread at the top.

Spread this slice with sandwich filling.
Continue to alternate the slices and spread
filling between. Press the layers together
so that the loaf will be firm. Cut crosswise
slices to obtain checkerboard sandwiches.
A perfect checkerboard design will be
obtained if all slices are of equal thickness and filling is spread
evenly.

Ribbon Sandwiches   Alternate slices
of light and dark bread which has been
spread with the same or different colored fillings. Use three or five slices in
each stack; press slices together firmly,
then slice. Cut ribbon sandwiches in
two or three parts if smaller sandwiches are desired.

Rolled Sandwiches   Use fresh bread
cut in thin, even slices. Remove crusts.
Spread with butter or other desired filling.
Roll, then fasten with toothpick and place
in refrigerator to set. Cut in crosswise
slices.

For variation, use three or more different fillings, place in
1-inch rows across the slice of bread, and roll slice so that
filling is in parallel lines with long edge of roll. When set, slice.

Soups

BACON Sprinkle tiny bacon curls, bits or shreds, over cream soup.

CHEESE Scatter grated Swiss or Parmesan cheese over soup.

Use cheese sticks, balls, rolls, or rings as soup accompaniments. Roll either yeast or quick-bread dough in grated cheese after shaping and before baking.

CHEESE PASTRIES Cut cheese pastry in shape of flowers, animals, or other objects. Bake and place on cream soups.

CHEESE POPCORN Serve with soup as an accompaniment.

CHICKEN LIVER BALLS Prepare forcemeat, using cooked chicken liver. Dip in slightly beaten egg, roll in cracker crumbs, and cook in chicken soup about 10 or 15 minutes. Place one on top of a sprig of parsley in each soup cup.

CREAM   Whip cream, and add a few grains of salt. Top soup with a spoonful of whipped cream just before serving. The whipped cream may be used plain, tinted to harmonize with soup, decorated with chopped parsley, chopped pimiento, sliced olive, or sprinkled with paprika, mace, or nutmeg. For variation, minced chives or truffles may be scattered over whipped cream.

CROUTONS   Cut day-old bread in shape of diamonds, tiny baskets (without handles), hearts, spades, or other shapes. Toast and serve on soup. Grated cheese may be sprinkled over croutons before toasting.

CUSTARD ROYALE   Bake custard about ½ inch thick in flat pan. Cut in fancy shapes and serve on cream soup.

EGGS   Sieve or finely chop hard-cooked egg white and yolk separately or together. Sprinkle over cream of tomato, pea, or other cream soup.

Slice hard-cooked egg and place on top of cream of asparagus or other colored soup.

Prepare egg balls and cook in soup, or deep-fat fry and add to soup just before serving. Egg balls may be made as follows: Force 2 hard-cooked egg yolks through a sieve, add ¼ teaspoon salt and a few grains of pepper. Add enough liquid egg white (about one egg white) to moisten. Shape in small balls about ¾ inch in diameter, roll in flour, and fry in deep fat or sauté in a small amount of fat until lightly browned. The uncooked balls may be dropped in the soup and cooked about 10 minutes before serving.

ENGLISH MUFFINS Prepare as croutons in the form of tiny molds or cutouts. Toast and serve on soup. Large pieces of whole muffins may be used as accompaniments.

HERBS Chop chives, parsley, chervil, basil, watercress, or rosemary. Sprinkle on soup.

ITALIAN PASTE Italian paste may be purchased cut in fancy shapes, such as seeds, stars, alphabet, musical notes, animals, crowns, shells, and flowers. Cook and serve in clear soups.

LEMONS Place a slice of lemon on the rim of a bowl of fish soup.

MEAT Place a few shreds of turkey, chicken, ham, or smoked meat in center of cream soup.

NUT MEATS Scatter chopped almonds, peanuts, or pistachios on cream soups.

OKRA Cook thin slices of okra in vegetable soup. Serve with slice of okra on surface.

OLIVES Place whole ripe olive in center of light-colored purée.

Chop ripe, green, or stuffed olives and place in ring formation on cream soups.

Slice stuffed olives and overlap three slices in a circle in center of cream soup.

ONIONS   Overlap two or three rings of parboiled onion on purées.

PASTRY STRIPS   Cut pastry in tiny strips. Serve plain or sprinkled with cheese or paprika.

PIMIENTO   Chop pimiento, or cut in fancy shapes, and place on soup with or without bits of truffle.

SAUSAGES   Use varieties of sausages or frankfurters. Cut sausage into fancy shapes; slice frankfurters. Heat and serve as garnish on soup.

SPICES   Sprinkle mace or paprika over soup.

TRUFFLES   Cut in design or scatter bits of truffle over soup.

VEGETABLES   Cut vegetables, such as carrots, turnips, or rutabagas in the shape of animals or other objects. Cook and serve on vegetable soup.

Ideas for Bed Trays

BOTH THE MOTHER in the home and the dietitian in the hospital are constantly looking for ideas to brighten the lives of the patients under their care. Whether young or old, patients appreciate a little thoughtfulness, and, regardless of age, enjoy the things they loved in childhood. Just a bit of color in the napkin, a different name or number card, a flower—all have a beneficial psychological effect and indirectly speed the recovery of the patient. There are many devices which require neither additional time nor artistic ability.

The dietitian in the hospital has no difficulty in selecting suitable food garnishes for her patients whether they are on restricted or regular hospital diets. It would be unwise, however, for the average lay person to garnish food for patients on restricted diets unless advised by a doctor or dietitian. Since food garnishes are usually edible, they may have undesirable reaction on the patient. It is better in such cases to brighten the tray with attractive name cards, favors, or place mats; or by the use of colorful dishes, napkins, and garden flowers.

Unrestricted Diets

As already mentioned, food garnishes may be used for invalids on unrestricted diets. Usually one attractive garnish on a tray is sufficient; two different kinds of garnishes may be used in the same service but not on the same food. More than two would give the tray a heavy and overworked appearance.

In each meal certain types of foods lend themselves to garnishing more than others. Breakfasts, which usually consist of fruit, cereal, a protein dish, breadstuff, and beverage can be served attractively through unusual preparation of the foods themselves or by means of garnishes applied to fruits and/or cereals.

Here are a few suggestions:

BREAKFAST

Applesauce   Sprinkle spice on top of sauce before serving, or top sauce with a few fresh or canned berries.

Berries, Cherries   Place a tiny, well-formed mound of powdered sugar in center of plate; arrange unhulled strawberries around the mound.

Sprinkle powdered sugar over berries.

Leave stems on cherries and arrange in clusters on plate.

Insert a tiny sprig of mint leaves in center of fruit, or arrange the leaves artistically near edge of dish.

Grapefruit   Cut grapefruit in half, separate segments, and place a red or green maraschino cherry in center. For variety, cut cherry in the shape of petals before placing on grapefruit. Serve with or without mint leaves.

Arrange fresh raspberries, blackberries, blueberries, or cherries (red or black) around center of grapefruit. Whole nut meats may be used in place of fruits.

Insert three peach slices or slices of red-skinned apple equidistant between grapefruit segments.

Oranges   Serve oranges with curled peel attached. To prepare, cut the skin into eight to ten lengthwise sections, beginning at the blossom end and cutting to the stem end. Loosen peel from each segment and curl, rolling peel inside toward orange. Roll peel down as far as possible without tearing from base of orange. Remove white membrane from orange pulp.

Cut orange peel into segments as described above. Instead of removing peel down to stem end, loosen each section at the top to simulate a budding flower.

Cut a ½-inch band around the middle crosswise portion of an orange; remove all peel except the band. Serve orange in this way, or make a crosswise cut through the band and open orange. Separate the segments and serve on plate with orange rind on the bottom.

Prunes   Serve with orange slice, either whole or cut in wedges.

Sprinkle grated orange or lemon rind on top of prunes.

Arrange orange or lemon rind cut in julienne strips on fruit before serving.

Fruit Juice   Serve in a different glass each morning.

Float a small slice of orange, lemon, or lime on juice in glass; top with a bit of maraschino cherry or tiny blossom.

Attach a small slice of orange, lemon, or lime to edge of serving glass; fasten a tiny sprig of green leaves to the slice of fruit.

Cereal   Top with fresh or canned berries, cherries, sliced fruit, such as peaches or bananas, dates, currants, or raisins.

LUNCHEONS usually consist of a cream soup, a protein or vegetable dish, breadstuff, salad, dessert, and beverage.

Soups may be garnished with sieved hard-cooked yolk of egg, minced olives, parsley, or pimiento.

Salads, crisp and colorful, lend a tempting note to any tray. They are a garnish in themselves.

Simple garnishes for **desserts** may take the form of sauces, chopped nuts, whipped cream, or fresh fruit, such as whole or crushed berries, sliced peaches, bananas, or oranges.

DINNERS may or may not begin with a soup. If they do, it is usually in the form of a clear broth, well seasoned. The dinner, in addition to the soup or hors d'oeuvres, would consist of a protein, a starchy vegetable, a green or other succulent vegetable, a simple salad, breadstuff, dessert, and beverage. Any one or two of the garnishes suggested in the preceding chapters may be used; they should, of course, harmonize and present a balanced appearance.

Restricted Diets

There are many ways in which a busy mother, wife, or nurse can add color to a tray when the food itself is restricted. Following are some suggestions.

NAME CARDS   Use old greeting cards to make stand-up pictures. Cut out the upper half of the picture, leaving the lower half intact. To form an easel, fold back the upper part of the card that has been cut away. Stand on tray.

Stick gummed labels on name cards, preferably in one corner of the card. Write name in free space.

NAPKINS Use decorative paper napkins—a different one for each meal: assorted solid colors, fancy borders, or designs to suit special occasions.

Fold napkins in different ways to add a note of interest, such as squares, rectangles, or triangles. To stand the triangular folded napkin, tuck one end of the base of the triangle into the folds of the other. Or fold the napkin to resemble an extended fan. First fold the napkin into a square, then tuck under each corner separately so that each fan-shaped fold lies higher than the preceding one. For variety, place a little flower near the edge of one fold.

DISHES Dishes of different colors and patterns may be combined with pleasing effects, if they are matched in texture: semi-porcelain with semi-porcelain, plastic with plastic, china with china, and glass with glass.

TRAY MATS Cloth mats with matching napkins lend dignity to any tray but may present a laundering problem. Paper, paper lace, plastic, or oilcloth mats can be purchased in various designs and colors.

FLOWERS Any flower, even colorful wild flowers, will enliven an otherwise dull, drab tray. Just a single blossom from the garden or from a potted plant can be placed on the napkin or in a tiny bud vase.

FAVORS Inexpensive favors for various occasions, such as flags for the Fourth of July, shamrocks for St. Patrick's Day, and valentines for St. Valentine's Day, can be purchased in novelty and department stores.

Suggestions for Holidays and Special Occasions

CHRISTMAS

Favors   Cut colored cellophane straws into 2-inch lengths. Tie a bundle of the straws together in the middle. Separate the ends of the straws to form a pompon and attach to a name card.

Decorate a 4- or 5-inch red or green candle with ribbon of opposite color. Set in a large gumdrop, a cork, or small square of styrofoam (plastic foam). If cork is used, cover with ruffled cellophane. Light just before entering the room. The candle may also be set in melted wax which has been allowed to harden on stiff, star-shaped paper. (Paper must be stiff enough to serve as a base.)

Make individual popcorn Christmas trees. Use popcorn in natural color or tint green by coloring the sirup with fruit or vegetable coloring, or spraying the corn after it has been popped. Decorate with bits of candied fruit or gumdrops in various colors. The trees can be formed around a wire frame. Insert wire at the bottom of the tree in paper-covered cork base.

Cut Christmas tree out of green paper. Using a paper punch, punch holes here and there on the branches, then paste colored paper over the back of the holes so that the colors will show through as different-colored ornaments. Two trees may be cut out together, colored paper pasted to the back of one, and the trees then pasted together. Fold the bases back in opposite directions to form a stand for the tree.

Stand a cutout angel or nativity scene in a cardboard support, a piece of styrofoam, or a tiny square of wood with a slit in center of top. Use paper that is stiff enough to stand.

Fashion a Santa Claus from a large red apple. Attach a marshmallow head with toothpicks; insert candy eyes and a red cherry mouth. With sirup, stick a border of cotton around the middle of the apple, pompons up and down the front, and a border around the neck to form a collar. Fasten a cotton mustache and beard to the face.

Dilute glue and spray on sprigs of balsam, fir, or pine. While wet, scatter grated or shredded bits of styrofoam over greens to resemble snow. Fasten twigs together with Ɪed ribbon.

Insert small birthday candles into white or tinted marshmallows. If the marshmallows are tinted, use candles of opposite color. Insert a Life Saver in the side of the marshmallow for a handle. These candles may be used as place cards. Paint the name on the side of the marshmallow, using pure fruit coloring and a paintbrush.

Food Edible red-and-green combinations

Parsley dipped in paprika.
Cream cheese on bread fingers with minced parsley and paprika.
Shredded red and green cabbage, marinated.
Beet relish served on fresh greens.
Hot tomato soup sprinkled with minced parsley.
Paprika and minced parsley on baked stuffed potatoes.
Red and green maraschino cherries on salads.
Red and green candied cherries on desserts.
Butter Stars: Cut brick butter into as many slices as needed, then cut each slice into stars (use star form or cardboard pattern). Place stars on individual plates.

NEW YEAR

Favors Place a white birthday candle in a cork which has been painted with silver paint. Cut out numbers to represent the New Year and paste on side of cork. Place cork and candle on mat of blue bells. To make blue bells, trace a circle of bells on blue paper in such a way that the top of the bells meet but do not overlap; cut bell tracings up to point of meeting.

Cut a star from stiff red or blue paper for base. Attach a fluted wire, about 4 inches long, to star base at one end and a colored paper name card at the other. Write name on name card.

Insert a white 4-inch to 6-inch candle in a styrofoam or clear plastic holder. Place on a glossy blue mat. Cut numbers corresponding to the year from paper similar to that used for the mat and fasten to the front of the base with paste, glue, or tiny pins.

Carve a snowball or other suitable object out of styrofoam. Insert a candle or decorate with ribbon and attach a name card.

Fashion a snowman from cotton. Use cloves for the eyes, a piece of red paper for the mouth, and a paper cup for the crown of the hat. Attach the features to the cotton with glue. Cut the brim from stiff paper to fit the crown. Tie a small colored kerchief around the neck and an apron to match around the waist. To give the hat a more finished look, place a band around the crown and tuck in a feather or artificial flower.

Food Form clock faces on top of frosted cupcakes by using angelica or strips of licorice.

Cut hard-cooked eggs in half lengthwise, remove yolks and fill whites with black and orange caviar, every other egg white being filled with an alternating color. Cut numbers from 1 to 12 out of turnip slices; place on top of caviar. The eggs should be arranged on the tray in clock fashion.

Write the name of the invalid on cookie bells with melted chocolate. Place in center of dessert, either flat or standing on end.

Form a snowman, using a frosted cupcake for the body and a marshmallow for the head. Use currants or raisins for eyes and a cherry for the mouth. Cap with a slice of a large gumdrop.

LINCOLN'S BIRTHDAY

Favors   Draw a log cabin in one corner of the name card.

Stencil, draw, or stick gummed pictures of squirrels or other wild animals and birds on stiff background paper cut in same shape as animal. Attach to colored toothpicks and stand in the name holder on tray.

Food   Serve strips of fudge, date, or Tootsie Rolls piled crisscross to resemble log-cabin or rail fence.

Use a 2½ to 3-inch cube of chocolate cake. Cut the top surface to form a peaked roof. With chocolate frosting fasten rectangular-shaped cookies to the slanting sides (or roof). The cookies should be the same size as the sides of the roof. Use a large gumdrop for the chimney and long, slender gumdrops or strips for the door and window frames.

Make small spongecake mallets by spreading thin slices of spongecake with chocolate frosting and rolling up like a jelly roll. Frost and cut into desired length. Insert stick of candy for a handle.

ST. VALENTINE'S DAY

Favors   Write the name of the patient across a heart-shaped card or valentine.

Use lace paper doilies as a nosegay. Place real flowers in center of ruffled doily or form flowers with different-shaped gumdrops attached to wire stems.

Stand a real flower in a heart-shaped styrofoam or plastic base.

Cut edges from lace paper doily and paste around outer rim of a red cardboard heart. Pierce heart with arrow cut from white construction paper.

Food Serve a Valentine dessert of heart-shaped meringues filled with strawberry ice cream. Stick a Cupid's-dart cookie into the ice cream.

Make heart-shaped cookies and sprinkle with red sugar.

WASHINGTON'S BIRTHDAY

Favors Buy or make tiny drums; leave one side open, and use as a nut or candy cup. To make drum, paste a rectangular piece of paper, decorated to resemble drum, around paper nut cup having straight sides.

Spray a few small twigs with green paint or dye and hang cellophane-covered red hard candy on branches to simulate cherries. A few fresh green leaves may be arranged among the cherries.

Place a 3-inch American shield on the tray. It should have a firm backing so that it will stand.

Either blow a raw egg out of its shell or cook egg until firm. Draw the features of Washington's face on the egg. Place a powdered (cotton) wig on top of the head. Stand in stiff paper collar.

Food Make cookies in the form of a log and hatchet combined. Decorate with candied cherries.

ST. PATRICK'S DAY

Favors Fasten shamrock stickers to white name cards. Write name in green ink.

Place tiny potted shamrocks on tray.

Tie a green ribbon on an Irish clay pipe. Place on green lace mat.

Stand pictures or cutouts of harps or Irish lads and lassies on the tray. Roll sheet music of Irish melodies and tie with a green ribbon.

Hollow out a marshmallow for the bowl of a pipe; insert a green stick-candy handle.

Food For an unrestricted diet, top pineapple slices with round molds of well-seasoned green vegetable salad in the shape of the crown of a hat. Spread softened cream cheese on top of the crown and place leaves of watercress around it. Serve on fresh greens.

Top salads with mint or lime gelatin cut in the shape of shamrocks.

Mold quick or yeast breads in shape of shamrocks and Irish pipes. Insert a strip of dough for the stem of the pipe before dough is baked.

EASTER

Favors Attach name card to tiny Easter basket. Simple baskets may be made by covering paper dishes with ruffled cellophane and attaching a pipe-cleaner handle. Fasten a tiny spray of flowers at the base of the handle. Metaloid fringe (metal-coated plastic) may be used around cup or other dish of suitable size. This makes a very effective basket. Metaloid comes in many colors. Glossy surfaced gift wrapping paper may also be used to make attractive baskets.

Trim Easter eggs in various ways. For example, paint a face on a hard-cooked egg. Make a hat or cap out of colored paper, then stand in stiff paper collar.

Draw and cut out a mother duck pulling a cart of baby ducks or colored eggs, using paper stiff enough to stand. Insert into slit cut in styrofoam base, or in a paper-covered wood base.

Draw a lily plant with leaves and container on stiff paper. Cut out and stand on tray.

Mold a nest with green-paper grass which can be purchased in the five-and-ten-cent stores. Arrange chocolate rabbits or downy chickens and nests of colored gumdrop eggs on the paper grass. Hard-coated candy eggs may be used instead of gumdrops.

Attach a rabbit face to one side of a nut cup. Use a slice of marshmallow for the nose and paper for the ears, head, and whiskers. Any colored, rather stiff construction paper may be used.

Food *Butter Flowers* Use a paring knife with a rounded end. Draw the knife lightly across the butter until there is as much as the knife can hold. Remove gently and form into a flower. Place on top of another pat of butter. Butter should be neither too hard nor too soft. Insert a bit of cherry, pimiento, carrot, or orange peel in center of flower. To color the flower, touch the edges with a cloth that has been dipped in brilliant red paprika.

Rabbit Easter Eggs Hard-cook eggs; cool. Remove shell. Use small gumdrop rings or truffle rings for the eyes, brown straws or twisted crepe paper for the whiskers. Paint or draw the nose and center of eyes with pure fruit coloring. Cut ears from white paper, crease down the center, and fasten in place with gummed transparent tape or insert two blanched

almonds for ears; paint a pink line down the center portion of each ear. Cut a slightly curved strip from heavy white paper for the stand. Print name across front of paper stand; fasten ends of paper together. Place the rabbit Easter egg on the stand.

Easter Chick Cut a marshmallow in half; dampen cut edges and fasten to sides of whole marshmallow. Cut gashes in marshmallow and insert candy corn for beak and tail. Draw eyes with fruit coloring. Use toothpicks for legs and gumdrops for feet.

Butter Lambs Butter lambs may be molded and placed in the refrigerator to chill before serving. Use bits of raisins for the eyes and cherry for the mouth. A banner with the word "Allelulia" lettered on it may be attached to a toothpick and inserted behind the head of the lamb. Lamb molds come in different sizes, some suited for butter molds, others for cake molds.

MAY–JUNE

Favors Make a little man out of gumdrops. Use two or three large gumdrops for the body; fasten with toothpicks. Place a large round gumdrop on end of toothpick for head; use three or four long gumdrops for legs and feet. Do the same for the arms. Curve the arms around some spring flowers. Place a small dried apricot hat on head of gumdrop man.

Use sprigs of apple blossoms on service plate at base of glass stemware in which appetizer or dessert is served.

Use forsythia sprays or other graceful flowers for grapefruit basket handles.

Arrange daisies around edge of service plate. An attractive effect can be produced with daisies by fastening their stems underneath the rim of the plate with gummed transparent tape.

FOURTH OF JULY

Favors Tie napkins with red, white, and blue ribbon.

Make firecrackers by wrapping thick stick candy in red cellophane with heavy cotton twine or a long shred of coconut for the fuse.

Write name of patient in white ink on red candy or nut-filled firecracker.

Place red carnation on white lace mat. Tie small bow of red, white, and blue ribbon to stem of flower.

Stand a cutout of Uncle Sam in name card holder. Write name of patient on band of hat.

Food Decorate cookies with red and blue colored sugar and sprinkle with silver candy decorations.

Cut liberty bells out of cookie dough. Use melted chocolate to mark crack in the bell.

HALLOWEEN

Favors Insert a small white or black candle in pumpkin candy base.

Fasten a paper cutout owl to a nut cup.

Buy or cut out clowns; stand in styrofoam base.

Make a gumdrop cat. Fasten two black gumdrops together with toothpicks for the body; attach another one for the head. Stick toothpicks through orange jelly beans and insert in body for legs and tail. Use strips of marshmallow for ears and toothpicks for whiskers.

Cut off top of an orange to form a small Jack-o'-lantern. Remove pulp. Cut eyes, nose, and mouth in orange shell with a pointed knife. Cut hole for small candle in bottom of shell. Insert piece of green pepper in top for stem.

Food Make a butter or margarine kitty. Shape butter or colored margarine into balls; drop into ice water to harden. Just before serving, cut chips from an apple peel for the eyes, ears, and nose. Make whiskers with shredded wheat.

Cover the outside of small ice-cream cones with chocolate icing or dipping chocolate. Place a scoop of ice cream on chocolate-iced cookies or cake rounds. Invert the cones over the ice cream. Make hatbands of sliced orange jelly or tangerine sections. Use raisins for eyes and nose and cherry section for mouth.

Cut a cat, pumpkin, or witch from pie dough, then bake and place on top of individual pies.

THANKSGIVING

Favors Construct a turkey by using a large gumdrop for the body, pipe cleaner for the neck and legs, and a small gumdrop for the head. Paper may be used for the bill and tail. Cut tail in shape of a large open fan.

Draw a picture of a Pilgrim child on stiff construction paper. Stand in name card holder.

Paste a horn of plenty in corner of name card.

Arrange colored leaves or fall flowers on napkin or serving tray.

Food Mold salads in turkey or pumpkin forms.

Cut rolled cookie dough in shape of Pilgrims, turkeys, and pumpkins.

The ideas and suggestions in this chapter may be used for table decorations as well as for trays.

Plate and Platter Arrangements

MANY FOODS combined in a course or meal will serve as garnishes by contrasting or complementing the color, texture, and form.

HOT PLATE SUGGESTIONS

Fried chicken
Julienne green beans
Lettuce cup containing a cran-
    berry-sauce chick on
    cheese-spread pineapple
    ring

Fried haddock with lemon
    sauce over watercress
Parsley potatoes
Whole-kernel corn
Head lettuce with dressing

Asparagus on whole-wheat
    biscuit topped with cheese
    sauce
Deviled eggs
Watercress

Macaroni and cheese in
    ramekin
Pickled figs
Cabbage slaw
Whole glazed carrots
Parsley

Swiss steak topped with
    broiled tomato and sautéed
    onion rings
Buttered carrot strips
Mashed potatoes and gravy
Parsley
Pineapple-apricot salad with
    Bing cherry in apricot
    cavity
Lettuce

Surprise veal birds (slices of
    veal rolled around cooked
    carrot sticks)
Scalloped potatoes
Lemon cup filled with currant
    or mint jelly
Lime gelatin fruit salad

Canned cured pork and beef
    loaf filled with fruit
    dressing
Strip of candied orange or
    grapefruit peel curved over
    meat
Asparagus with butter-
    browned almonds
Hot baking-powder biscuits
    with jelly

Salmon-stuffed pepper
Asparagus topped with
    pimiento strip
Buttered carrots
Ripe olives
Parsley

Round biscuit, split, topped
    with slice of cheese and
    toasted
Slice of onion
Poached egg
Watercress
Parsley

Parsley potatoes
Fried oysters
Tartar sauce on lettuce
Asparagus topped with white
    sauce and strip of pimiento

Chicken croquettes
Spiced peach in bed of water-
    cress
Green and ripe olives
Creamed peas on Holland
    rusk

COLD PLATE SUGGESTIONS

Canned pineapple slice
Ripe bananas
Salad greens
Fresh raspberries, grapes, or
    cherries

Red-skinned apple slices
Orange slices cut in half
Strawberries
Chicory (curly endive)
Ripe banana

Free-stone peach half
Quarters of unpeeled Bartlett pear
Red raspberries
Orange slices
Head lettuce, romaine, or endive (Serve in colored pottery bowl if available)

Potato salad in lettuce cup
Deviled eggs
Tomato slices
Whole-wheat bread
Cucumber slices
Ripe olives
Spiced crabapples

Tomato aspic cubes in lettuce cup sprinkled with sieved egg yolk
Small whole carrots
Two or three cold cuts
Cooked peas, cubed cheese, and dressing mixed and served in lettuce cup
Toasted English muffin topped with parsley cottage cheese or savory butter

Sliced canned pineapple topped with shrimp
Radish roses
Cold cuts
Slices of pepper stuffed with cottage cheese
Salad dressing
Green olives

Half-inch slice of head lettuce topped with slice of cranberry jelly
Chicken salad
Deviled eggs
Marinated asparagus tips
Ripe and green olives

Jellied peach half filled with cottage cheese
Avocado slices and orange sections standing next to each other in bed of watercress
Half banana cut lengthwise
Berries and grapes
Hot, thin biscuits with grilled bacon

Tomato stuffed with cottage cheese
Coleslaw
Sliced cucumber
Radish roses
Scallions
Deviled egg
Ham loaf
Potato chips
Ripe olives

Melon balls and berries
Orange and grapefruit sections
Prunes stuffed with cottage cheese
Toasted ham sandwiches

Cheese-stuffed jumbo prunes
Banana fingers
Two canned cling peach
*   halves*
Lettuce or endive

PLATTER ARRANGEMENTS

Macaroni and cheese
Broiled tomato slices on toast
*   rounds*

Macaroni, cheese, and
*   vegetable ring*
Salmon white sauce
Parsley

Fried chicken
Buttered green beans in onion
*   ring*
Tomato slices
Parsley

Calavo pears cut in half and
*   filled with diced cooked*
*   chicken, celery, and*
*   peppers in white sauce*
Butter crackers
Curly endive

Chicken croquettes
Cranberry sauce in lemon
*   cups*
Lattice potatoes
Parsley

Croquettes wrapped in bacon
*   strips*
Sliced hard-cooked eggs
*   sprinkled with paprika*
Lemon sections
Parsley

Salisbury steak
Stuffed tomatoes
Onion slices dipped in fritter
*   batter and deep-fat fried*

Individual ham loaves
Whole buttered green beans
*   topped with strips of*
*   pimiento*
Parsley potato balls
Sprigs of parsley

Individual meat loaves
Sweet-potato nests filled with
*   buttered peas*
Turnip flowers

Rice mold with bacon curls
Cheese sauce in center dish
Parsley

Pork link sausages
Sweet-potato rounds (dented
  in center) covered with
  crumbled corn flakes and
  filled with cranberry or
  other jelly
Parsley

Stuffed frankfurters
Sliced tomatoes
Curly endive
Cabbage salad

Deviled noodles
Frankfurter ring
Parsley
Radish roses

Luncheon braid filled with
  ground meat mixture
  (Braid may be made with
  baking-powder biscuit
  dough, patty shell dough,
  or pastry)
Radish roses
Parsley
Peach and cottage cheese
  salad topped with cherry

Rice diamond-shaped mold
  with shrimp creole (Garnish mold with shrimp and
  creole sauce and pimiento
  strips or pimiento cut in
  shape of diamonds)

Rice mold surrounded with
  cooked carrots and peas
  and topped with egg-white
  rings filled with buttered
  peas and sprinkled with
  sieved egg yolk

Olive rice ring filled with
  creamed green string beans
Ripe olives
Parsley
Tomato and curly endive
  salad

Red and white cabbage rice
  ring mold filled with
  creamed cubed carrots
Cubed carrot border with
  radish roses and parsley

Omelet with parsley, served
  with creamed tuna, lobster,
  chicken, or vegetables

Egg pancakes served with
  fruit sauce and struesel
  topping

Cabbage shell (inside portion
  removed from cabbage
  head) filled with meat balls
  and tomato sauce
Carrot slices and parsley
  butter

Creamed eggs and shrimp in toast cups sprinkled with crushed toasted dry soybeans
Buttered peas
Parsley

Vegetable macédoine consisting of
Sliced peeled tomatoes
Sliced radishes
Carrot sticks
Cooked peas
Sliced unpeeled cucumber
Halves of hard-cooked egg
Green onions
Salad dressing
Lettuce

Green string beans and onion slices topped with cubed meat in tomato sauce
Parsley

Stuffed baked potatoes (force whipped potatoes through pastry tube) filled with creamed vegetables or fish

Cold cuts consisting of
Bologna
Old-fashioned meat loaf
Fresh pineapple shell filled with mixed fresh fruit
Parsley

Sliced tongue
Stuffed olives in lettuce cups
Radish roses in parsley beds
Tomato sections
Lettuce

Chicken noodle loaf
Jumbo prunes
Whole spiced peaches
Curly endive

Sliced meat loaf
Pear halves on orange slices filled with mint jelly and red cherries
Parsley

Cold meat platter consisting of
Bologna cornucopias stuffed with cottage cheese flavored with onions
Braunschweiger slices
Sliced cooked ham
Watercress
Radish roses

Peppered meat loaf
Macaroni-and-cheese loaf
Liver cheese
Tomato shells filled with small pickles, pickled onions, thin slices of cervelat at outer edge
Parsley
Carrot curls

Salami slices
Cheese cubes *filled with
colored toothpicks*
Deviled eggs *filled with
Braunschweiger liver
sausage mixed with salad
dressing, horse-radish, and
egg yolk*
Parsley

Assorted cold cuts
Bologna *stuffed with cottage
cheese*
Flowers *made from carrot
strips and ripe olive centers
(cut carrot strips about 1
inch wide and shape like
petals)*
Parsley

Cornucopias *made from
rolled meat slices and
stuffed olives*
Braunschweiger *slices*
Pickles
Radish *roses*
Ripe *olives*
Parsley
Celery *curls and carrot fringe*

Shrimp salad loaf
Watercress
Celery *hearts*
Red *radishes*
Pickled *onions*
Ripe *and green olives*
Sweet *pickles*

Egg salad and vegetable
combination loaf
Chicken and pineapple *loaf
topped with almonds*
Molded macaroni and cheese
*loaf topped with sliced
stuffed olives*
Salmon mousse *topped with
cucumber slices*

Cottage cheese
Sliced *cucumbers*
Tomato *wedges*
Carrots *cut with fluting knife*
Onion *rings*
Green *pepper rings*

Pork chops *topped with sweet
potato and spiced prune*
Radish *roses*
Parsley

Lamb roast
Mashed potato nests *filled
with buttered peas and
sautéed mushrooms*
Lemon *or orange slices
topped with mint jelly*

Yellow tomatoes *(or persim-
mons) topped with toasted
marshmallows*
Fried *chicken*
Parsley
Radish *roses*

*Small head of red cabbage
    filled with salad dressing
Orange slices
Red raspberries
Strawberries
Fresh figs
Boysenberries
Mint leaves
Curly endive*

*Baked stuffed fish
Boiled rice
Cucumber slices
Stuffed olives cut in half
Lemon sections
Parsley*

*Codfish topped with white
    sauce and egg slices
Lemon wedges
Parsley
Parsley potatoes
Whole onions*

*Halibut steaks
Meat patties topped with
    onions
Broiled tomatoes
Ginger rolls
Parsley
Radish roses*

*Planked halibut steak topped
    with fancy lemon slices and
    pimiento strips
Peas in beet cups
Mashed potatoes formed in
    cones with pastry tube
Parsley*

*Baked stuffed haddock topped
    with overlapping lemon
    wedges or slices
Peas in paper cups
Glazed whole carrots
Parsley*

Index